"Stop chasing and start attracting. A must read for those who are ready to acknowledge that the key to your business is relationships."

LOU CASSARA

Author of *From Selling to Serving: The Essence of Client Creation*

"At long last, someone tells you the right things to do. These prospect attraction strategies deliver results. Guaranteed!"

TOM GUZZARDO

President, Guzzardo Leadership Group, Business Development Coach, Co-Author of *Success is a Team Effort*

"This book is your practical guide to turning yourself into a referral-generating machine."

BILL CATES

Author of *Get More Referrals Now*

"If you are ready to implement the strategies found between the covers of this book, buckle your seatbelt for your ascent to a higher level of sales success. This is a winner!"

BOB HOLTZCLAW

Guzzardo Leadership Group, Senior Performance Coach

"Solid advice on how to become a successful producer."

W.L. SEAWELL, II

Senior VP Marketing, Jefferson Pilot Financial

"Yesterday's selling techniques simply don't work. Becoming a 'little bit famous' is the prospect's new requirement. If you want big increases in sales, you must read this book."

JAMES HASSETT, Ph.D.

Author of *AdverSelling®: How to Build Stronger Relationships and Close More Sales by Applying 26 Principles from Successful Ad Campaigns*

"Cutting edge insights into prospect attraction! This book cuts through the typical generic marketing mumbo-jumbo. The depth of practical ideas is masterful."

MARK HILLMAN, Ph.D.

Award Winning Author of *My Therapist Is Making Me Nuts!*

"Proven ideas that will produce BIG RESULTS!"

JERRY STILLWELL

Senior VP and CMO, Lafayette Life Insurance Company

"Let's face it. Most financial service professionals fail. Why? Because they don't know how to market themselves. Read this book and you'll know a lot more about attracting clients."

RON WILLINGHAM

Author of *Integrity Selling for the 21st Century*

"It's about time every financial professional had access to this formula for success. This is proven, success-building information that can show you how to accomplish twice as much with half the effort."

LYLE GARY

Publisher, Agent Media Corporation – Insurance Selling magazine

"Read this book. It tells you what today's prospect really wants - an insight that has changed dramatically over the last few short years."

RICHARD R. SANDERSON, CLU, ChFC

National Business Development Director Nationwide Financial Services

Please...Make ME
a little bit
FAMOUS!

by Robert E. Krumroy

Please...Make ME
a little bit
FAMOUS!

Robert E. Krumroy

Author of
Identity Branding – Creating Prospect Attraction
and
Brilliant Strategies and Fatal Blunders

This publication may not be reproduced, stored in a retrieval system, or transmitted in whole or in part, in any form or by any means, electronic, mechanical, photocopying, recording, or otherwise, without the prior written permission from Robert E. Krumroy, president, Identity Branding, Inc., 2007 Yanceyville Street, Box 2, Greensboro, NC 27405. E-mail at info@identitybranding.com or call 336-303-7316.

Please... Make ME a little bit FAMOUS ©2006 by Robert E. Krumroy

Publish date: January 1, 2006

Given the current legal environment, we suggest that you consult your compliance or legal advisors before adapting the ideas presented in this book. We have not intentionally included any advice or materials that put you at risk, but we also realize how quickly and often laws and regulations change regarding the financial services industry.

All rights reserved. No part of this publication may be reproduced, stored in a retrieval system, or transmitted, in any form or by any means, electronic, mechanical, photocopying, recording, or otherwise, without the prior written permission of the copyright holder.

This publication is designed to provide accurate and authoritative information in regard to the subject matter covered. It is sold with the understanding that neither the author nor the publisher is engaged in rendering legal, accounting, or other professional service. If legal advice or other expert assistance is required, the services of a competent professional person should be sought.

From a Declaration of Principles jointly adopted by a committee of the American Bar Association and a Committee of Publishers.

I-B Publishing, Greensboro, NC
ISBN: 0-9678661-2-X

Printed in Canada

Contents

Please... Make ME a little bit FAMOUS

Dedicated to…

The men and women financial advisors who deliver
exceptional local market experiences;
whose uniqueness is so highly noticeable that they have
become a little bit famous.

Please... Make ME a little bit FAMOUS

Acknowledgements

My sincere thanks to the many people who made this book a reality. I am grateful to all of them for their knowledge and wisdom. Some brought lessons; others brought experiences; others gave their expertise. All made an impact on this book.

Brad Whitmore – Executive Vice President of Sales and Marketing. You are a great continuous resource whose input is invaluable. Thank you for your dedication and friendship.

Michelle Polczynski – Vice President of Operations. You have been a bastion of confidence and capability in my life. Thank you for the years of trust and loyalty. I look forward to many more.

Alan Polczynski – Director of Training. Our organization would never be as good as it is without you. You continue to give an extraordinary contribution to our clients. It never goes unnoticed.

Vanya Reed – Senior Customer Service Representative. Thank you for your thoroughness, coupled with the laughter and patience you always display. Even our customers go away smiling because of their encounter with you.

Renee Baber – Accounts Receivable Manager. Thank you for never just doing the job, but for always going the extra mile. Your daily, bubbly personality is always refreshing. It is a gift to all of us.

Ryan Baber – Our Invaluable Intern. We only wish we could clone you and hasten your college degree. Your ability to quickly learn and support our clients is remarkable. You are a real part of our team!

Betty Work –The best book editor in the world...and that is not an exaggeration.

Bill Heroy – The best professional photographer in the Southeast. A master at book covers, photos, and oil portraits.

Marian Stewart – The graphic design professional who continues to put up with my countless changes and maintains a smile.

Our computer tech people for burning the midnight oil and staying on top of our e-Relationship application.

And a special thanks to all our clients! Your weekly calls are always welcomed. Your success stories inspire all of us. Your willingness to share your experiences is our best teacher. We are eternally grateful. It is our honor to serve you.

Sincerely,
Robert E. Krumroy, CEO, Identity Branding, Inc.

Forward

Marketing. What's worked in the past, isn't working today. That's particularly relevant in the financial services industry. If you're a financial advisor doing the same things that you were doing three short years ago, then you are out-of-touch. Some prospects are ignoring you. Many of your clients may be indifferent. You're working harder to stay even and your frustration is escalating. What's gone wrong? Here are just a few observations:

• Most financial sales professionals don't manage prospect relationships in ways that build market affection.

• Most financial sales professionals have neither created nor are they managing an effective local attraction strategy.

• Most financial sales professionals have irrelevant or deficient market-differentiation.

• Most financial sales professionals still place more weight on process than people.

AND NO ONE IS TELLING YOU THE RIGHT THINGS TO DO DIFFERENTLY!

To make matters worse, the problem is more than a marketing issue. It is an imagination deficit problem. Most marketing in the financial industry is directed by sales or advertising departments, reducing marketing to brochures, selling systems, sales literature, and media advertising – none of which is helping the sales professional increase personal local attraction or build local market preference.

The emphasis of this book is to refocus your efforts on the right strategies; to make you market attractive; prospect appealing; help you stand out from the crowd; and to make YOU a little bit famous. Will it work? Get ready for BIG RESULTS. This book is a masterpiece. It should become your guide for building prospect attraction and deep client loyalty.

Ivan R. Misner, Ph.D.
Founder of BNI
Author of *Masters of Success*

Please... don't tell me about our newest product...
not again!

And don't tell me about our company's superior
industry ratings.

Don't just tell me to get better focused.

Don't tell me to get more committed to my
personal goals.

Don't just tell me to see more people.

Tell me how to become a little bit famous...LOCALLY!

THAT is what I want.

Becoming a little bit famous is a powerful strategy.

I was told...

Build it. They will come.

Robert E. Krumroy

Please... Make ME a little bit FAMOUS

la·gniappe \\'lan-,yap, lan-'yap
An extra or unexpected ingredient

"Lagniappe is what you do that makes you a little bit famous. It is that extra item that positions you as more special than the competition. In local market attraction, the extra item is always about people – not product, not process, not company affiliation. What's your unexpected ingredient?"

Please… Make ME a little bit FAMOUS

Chapter One

What I Learned at the Drugstore When I Was Six Years Old

Saturday arrived. My allowance, twenty-five cents, was always the highlight of the day. As predictable as the sun rising every morning, I would jump on my bicycle and pedal furiously five blocks to the corner drugstore and watch alertly outside the door until a certain clerk was available. When she was, I would dash in, put my nickel on her counter and request a quarter-pound of jawbreakers. From the big glass container, she scooped exactly four ounces of jawbreakers onto the scale… and then with a smile, she would dip into the jar and pluck out one more.

Six years old. Not a lot of years to understand marketing, pricing, packaging or competition. But I did understand that this clerk stood out from the rest. Everyone in my world knew her, and we diligently steered others to her counter. She was the clerk who gave customers a little bit extra. In return, she had become "a little bit famous."

Maybe you have similar childhood memories. Remember the place where they made milkshakes in a blender… and after filling your glass, they put what was left over in a side cup for you to enjoy? Or the place where they mixed cherry fountain cokes... and put two cherries on top, not just one. There's a word for this: lagniappe.

la·gniappe \'lan-,yap, lan-'yap\
1. *That little something extra that was never expected.*
2. *An extra or unexpected gift, effort or benefit that made the encounter superior to what was expected.*

In short, lagniappe is what you do that makes you more special than the competition. And in marketing, it is always about people over product.

The average person has an average routine. You get up, brush your teeth, take a shower, get dressed, have coffee, drive to work, have lunch at one of maybe three regular places, drive home, have dinner, read the paper, watch some TV, go to bed and then start over.

In a society like ours, it doesn't take much to create a local market impact that builds huge attraction. It just takes some simple thinking. A little strategy to create a positive emotional experience that stays in your prospect's mind.

What do you do that creates remarkable encounters for the important people in your life?

By important people, we are talking about prospects. They are the people who will drive your success... or, conversely, your mediocrity or failure. If you want great success, your job is to become great at consistently delivering lagniappe – that little something extra that can make YOU a little bit famous.

"Make ME a little bit FAMOUS" Notebook

My thoughts on how to apply this chapter's lessons to my business…

_____

_____

_____

_____

_____

_____

_____

_____

_____

_____

_____

_____

_____

_____

_____

_____

_____

_____

_____

_____

_____

_____

_____

_____

"Unique experiences provide the story material that your prospects and clients enthusiastically spread to others.

What's yours?"

Robert E. Krumroy

Chapter Two

It's Not Who YOU Know.
It's Who Knows YOU.

Take a journey with me to 1970. Insurance companies are selling insurance products. Brokerage houses are selling investments. Banks are performing their banking functions. Nobody interferes with the others' product distribution. Company name recognition is king. Sales reps only need courage, a good telephone script, a business card and a brochure to get their foot in the door.

This worked back then because competition was slim and there were plenty of prospects for everyone. It took just a little perseverance to get appointments.

Oddly (and unfortunately), many companies today are still throwing most of their marketing efforts into logos, corporate advertising, brochures, new products and Web sites. Is it working? Is it assisting local advisors in their efforts to get more appointments? I think we all know the answer.

Inflation hit consumers hard in the 1970s, making it very apparent that they needed to invest, not just save, their money. They knew they needed more security for their families and they had an increasing interest in things like mutual funds, additional life insurance and reducing taxes.

It was the beginning stages of financial planning. There were lots of eager prospects. The old patriarchal companies with their lifetime employees and big retirement pension payments were quickly fading. People accepted requests to sit down and discuss financial planning and investment ideas, and company name recognition mattered.

By the late 1970s to early 1980s, the leading financial companies realized they needed to adjust their marketing methods. Most confused marketing with selling, but the changes they made were still positive. They began transitioning their sales forces away from memorized sales talks and into consultative selling that got prospects more involved in their own needs-discovery processes and purchasing decisions.

This was a significant change, but it was **not** marketing – contrary to what many marketing directors still believe in many financial institutions. Selling systems are not attraction marketing tools.

By the mid-1980s, competition increased significantly as new laws allowed banks, stockbrokers and insurance companies to cross-product sell. Everyone sold everything. Historically high interest rates forced companies to create lots of new products. The emphasis became "new-better-performing-products." Unlike today, it only required a slight amount of personal moxie to get appointments and make sales.

By the late 1980s, as most financial products began looking more similar than dissimilar to consumers, the new market focus became "quality service." It wasn't long, however, before good service became the consumer's expectation instead of an initial market attractor. You gave good service or you lost customers.

So where do we stand today? Well, it should be pretty plain that attraction marketing is no longer about your company's product advantage, your selling system, your referral system, your quality service, or your company's name recognition. What it is about is creating a successful local prospect-attraction strategy – one that delivers a unique experience about YOU to your prospects and clients that they enthusiastically spread to others. That kind of prospect attraction is what intensifies client relationships and causes YOU to become a little bit famous.

Unlike selling, attraction marketing does not occur in the first face-to-face encounter (although, if done correctly, it makes that encounter easier to get and easier to sell). Attraction marketing is about what you do before the appointment.

Creating prospect attraction requires that you communicate frequently and consistently in ways that heighten your likeability and promote your personal business differentiation – differentiation that is people oriented, not product oriented. To maximize your ability to get prospects to enthusiastically accept a request to meet with you, the prospect must conclude that the unique experience you offer, not your company or your product, is exceptionally different and appealing.

Don't wait around for your company to teach you how to do this. Chances are, they can't and they won't, because they don't get it. They will continue to come up with new brochures, new products, maybe a new logo, and brag about their new television commercial. But none of these elements is going to affect local prospect attraction.

If you wish to succeed, you must take a very different course. The prospect audience has changed. It is time to respond. Prospect attraction is no longer about who you know. It is about who knows you.

"Make ME a little bit FAMOUS" Notebook

My thoughts on how to apply this chapter's lessons to my business…

_____
_____
_____
_____
_____
_____
_____
_____
_____
_____
_____
_____
_____
_____
_____
_____
_____
_____
_____
_____
_____
_____
_____
_____
_____

"An effective attraction strategy must
deliver YOU over and over and over
to your audience."

Robert E. Krumroy

Chapter Three

The New Prospect Attraction Model. Say Hello To PACC.

Your initial attraction in the local market has less to do with what you sell than it does with who you are.

When we meet people, it's only natural to try to identify a connection or a commonality. We ask what they do, where they live, where they're from. Maybe their child goes to your child's school. Perhaps they know someone you know.

We search. We question. We prod. When they answer affirmatively, we immediately feel a bond. We feel safe. The barriers go down. The trust goes up. We just discovered a commonality, which is the beginning step of bonding. It's the same first step required for initiating successful prospect attraction. Here's a brief introduction to PACC, the four steps you will follow to success. Each will be discussed in detail in the following chapters.

P – Prospect Database
Identify those people with whom you have developed (or can develop) a personal, social or belief connection and use their names to create a significant prospect database. If you can't

develop a meaningful connection with your selected group or groups, find a new market audience.

A – Activating Events

To maximize your local market attraction, you must create heightened awareness through multiple strategic encounters that are easily seen by local prospects and your clients. Positioning these events as ongoing experiences creates distinctive market separation, likeability and consistency.

C – Characteristic Uniqueness

Creating a reason for someone to give you an appointment requires that the prospect can conclude you have a distinctive business characteristic uniqueness, one that clients willingly and enthusiastically spread to others. Your business characteristic uniqueness should deliver a unique experience as compared to the typical competition, one that impacts both clients and people who haven't even met you.

C – Consistent Contact

In any industry, the person who is most frequently seen is always granted the subconscious title of highest expert in their field of endeavor. Frequent and ongoing communication is the single greatest element for creating market separation, accentuating your professional business image. If you're not seen frequently enough, prospects won't know what you do, existing clients will wander off, appointment activity will suffer, and you will even shy away from asking for referrals, knowing that your promise of staying in touch is more fiction than fact. A single piece of communication to a prospect, or a once-a-year connection to a client, is inadequate to establish trust, much less create and maintain a relationship. Your communication strategy must be frequent and ongoing (twelve to eighteen times a year) in order to keep clients and attract prospects.

Prospect Attraction Model
(PACC)

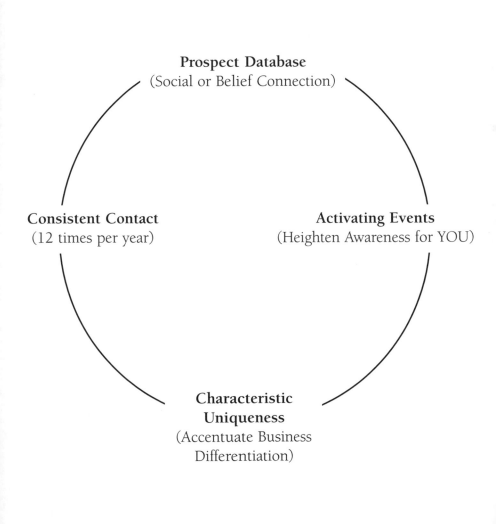

Prospect Database
(Social or Belief Connection)

Consistent Contact
(12 times per year)

Activating Events
(Heighten Awareness for YOU)

**Characteristic
Uniqueness**
(Accentuate Business
Differentiation)

Why the "Old Rules" Don't Work

Ignoring the four steps of prospect attraction keeps most financial advisors from producing at their talent level. Most are still being taught, by their primary companies and managers, these old rules for success:

1. Identify a prospect.
2. Be persistent enough to get an appointment.
3. Maneuver yourself into a sales process and get the order.

The old rules are devoid of attraction skills that help deliver us to our audience. The average desired prospect has little or no market awareness of us – and certainly no identifiable competitive preference.

It hasn't always been that way. In the 1950s, we were a less mobile society. We had limited business interaction and limited produce choice. But by the 1970s, we had evolved into a product society. Today the choices are so mind-boggling we extend our goodwill only to those who we believe embrace our value commonality. It's our way to withdraw from the over-stimulation of too many people attempting to get our money.

The impact is that appointment requests are met with ever-greater resistance these days. It's hard to get in. (Skeptical? Over seventy percent of America has signed up for the "Do Not Call" list. Chances are you have, too.)

Unless your local consumers have (1) a pre-awareness of "who you are," (2) can conclude that they would probably "like you" if they met you, and (3) believe that the package you offer (mostly YOU) is characteristically different from what they have witnessed from your industry, they aren't going to meet with you. Some will, but not the majority. You won't get the number of appointments you want, and you won't get the number of referrals you want.

It's no mystery to me why most advisors have an activity problem or a problem getting in to see new prospects. They simply have no strategy for delivering themselves to their market. It is your job to give prospective clients a way to get to **know** you, **like** you and **trust** you – the three elements people need before agreeing to sacrifice their precious time for a meeting.

Please… Make ME a little bit FAMOUS

"Make ME a little bit FAMOUS" Notebook

My thoughts on how to apply this chapter's lessons to my business...

_____

_____

_____

_____

_____

_____

_____

_____

_____

_____

_____

_____

_____

_____

_____

_____

_____

_____

_____

_____

_____

_____

_____

_____

_____

_____

_____

_____

"Stop believing that identifying a target market and then showing up in their midst is going to create prospect attraction and welcomed access for you.
This is just a basic start.
Nothing more."

Robert E. Krumroy

Chapter Four

The PACC Model
• Step One •

Prospect Database

Who is your prospect community?

It's not who you think. Unless your town is smaller than ten thousand people, your local community is not your prospect community. But somewhere in your local community or city, your prospect community resides – the one in which you can become a little bit famous.

Creating prospect attraction starts with a very small initial decision: defining a general group of people you want to target, such as Chamber of Commerce members, small-business owners in specific occupations, or people with income or net worth above a certain level. But be warned, this is just a basic start, nothing more. A general definition will get you nowhere if you end your strategy here.

Once you define your general target audience, you will need to get specific. You will find their names and insert them into a prospect database; you will begin a courting strategy that will give you a high profile; and then you will measure the success of your efforts.

Getting actual names for a database is an easy first step, taking only a small amount of time. But it is the precursor to delivering your professional business image in delightful ways and opening doors to new prospects.

There are six rules for attraction marketing discussed throughout this book that will help you in your endeavors. The first two rules are included in this chapter because they address where you should go to find names for your database.

The Rule of Social Commonality

How it works.
We like people who are similar to us. When meeting someone, we search for social commonality. We ask about backgrounds, interests, common friends, birthplaces, alma maters, church affiliations, occupational connections, civic groups, sports, hobbies, you name it. Our feeling of trust increases with our degree of social commonality.

The lesson.
When deciding which prospect community you want to become a little bit famous in, first consider organizations with which you already have a commonality. People connect with us when they feel we value what they value. When people perceive that we value them, they value us as well. Quoting Jerry Acuff and Wally Wood in *The Relationship Edge in Business:* "Finding common ground is not chitchat. There is a reason for it. The more common ground you find, the deeper the relationship is likely to be."

Identify friends and acquaintances with whom you share a connection. These people are frequently overlooked for fear that mixing friendship with business would be an unwelcome gesture, a relationship conflict. That is an unfortunate and bad conclusion. These people would actually be your most vocal fans and easiest clients if you heightened your reputation by consistently delivering and accentuating a professional business image. Let these people know what you do and remind them frequently with repeated connections.

Go to where your heart is. Do you belong to a church or synagogue? Are you active in an organization that has a passion for a specific cause? If you share beliefs with members of an existing group, don't ignore them as a primary prospect audience. No one is going to be offended. Why would you not want to become a little bit famous in a group that already embraces you? Remember: The point of the prospect-attraction strategy is not to organize names into a hit list but to pursue your objectives through experiential encounters that are relevant and likeable.

I'm often amazed at how many advisors are extremely well thought of in their churches, synagogues or charities, and yet members have only a very general idea of what they do. Agents, advisors and stockbrokers who belong to a mega-church, the Chamber of Commerce or a civic club... *and yet fail because they have nobody to call on?* This is a tragedy.

Even if you're already a success, you probably have lots of acquaintances who don't know what you do or don't remember what you do. This applies to clients, too. To be candid, clients don't remember what you do for more than a week after you tell them. How often have you heard, "I've known you for years. I knew you were in the insurance or financial business, but I never knew what you did." Applying an attraction strategy is not a one-time event and it isn't just for prospects. Building and maintaining shelf life in the minds of prospects and clients is a continuous process.

The Rule of Mutual Association

How it works.
We extend liking and trust to people with whom we have the most connection. Mutual association increases connection, commonality, affection and preference.

The lesson.
Every financial or insurance professional should belong to at least one formal group of people they want as clients. No greater connection with prospects occurs than being a fellow member of an organization or association. Identify groups in which you have a genuine interest, join them, and become actively involved. If you were the city executive at your local bank, you would be told to join the Rotary (lots of business owners) and the homebuilder's association (continuous need for money loans) or you would lose your job. Banks may be horrible at marketing, but they do know that mutual association creates a lot of business opportunities.

Joining isn't enough, though. As a member of an organization, you can't just stand on the sidelines, proclaiming your genuine connection and think that you will become appreciated and a little bit famous. Get relevantly involved with your church or synagogue, the Chamber of Commerce, the Human Resource Association, the Homebuilder's Association, the National Association of Women Business Owners, the Manufacturing Association, the International Trade Association, the Textile Association, the Yarn and Hosiery Association, the Furniture Association, or some other group that has structure, meetings and opportunities to become a visible STAR! (More about effective strategies later.)

Choose a sizable organization, one with at least two hundred fifty members. Here are some personal favorites where relationships and business are compatible.

Homebuilder's Association. The group is always large, meets monthly, is usually profitable, and welcomes associate members. Homebuilder's also are easy people to get referrals from – after all, that's how they're accustomed to doing business.

Pest Control Owners. The average pest control company owner makes a six-figure income and employs more than nine people. The economy has little effect on their profits; their product is always in demand. Their groups welcome outside members.

Human Resource Association. If you're trying to work with business owners, this is the group for you. They control company benefit plans and have access to the owners. They also control retirement plans and have tremendous influence on guiding retirees to places where they should place rollover funds from 401k's.

Plastic/Rubber Mold Injection Association. Member companies mold key chains, plastic coffee cups (used by Starbucks), novelties for company giveaways, computer shells, CD shells, etc. They typically employ thirty-five to fifty employees and the owners' average annual income exceeds a quarter of a million dollars – *conservatively estimated.* Most sizable cities have a couple hundred members within fifty miles, and these groups welcome associate members. Bankers are often members, building relationships so they can develop market preference in lending money for expansion in this fast-growing industry.

Chamber of Commerce. Chambers were created to promote business in the community, and they still encourage members to do business with fellow members. Their directories are the easiest source for quality prospects and the organization lends itself to becoming involved in high-profile events, such as annual golf tournaments. This is a source for any financial professional who wants to quickly uncover at least five hundred names for a prospect database.

Merchants Association. Similar to the Chamber of Commerce, but focused on retail.

National Association of Women Business Owners. It is estimated that women own fifty-three percent of businesses in the United States. Enough said. This is a not-to-miss opportunity.

There are hundreds of other groups that welcome associate members: landscapers, restaurant owners, HVAC, female contractors, manufacturing, textiles, furniture and more. Go to your public library and ask to see the local association directory; it will have all the particulars about associations you might be interested in: their focus, size of membership, officers, meeting times, and web address.

You can also use an Internet search engine like www.whitepages.com to get information that may help determine if a particular category of business is significant enough in size to consider as a preferred target. In the "Business Type" search box, type in the occupational grouping you are considering as a target market. The listings provide the number of businesses in that category, their addresses and phone numbers, and sometimes also e-mail addresses and owners' names. If you conclude that this is a desirable occupational market and want more information, call the company and request it. Tell them you specialize in their type of business and would like to e-mail them some information about the services you offer. Be confident. They will give you the information ninety percent of the time. (The other ten percent of the time, they will at least ask more questions while on the phone, leading to an opportunity for you to request a luncheon meeting.)

I would be remiss if I didn't also mention civic organizations. I believe every advisor should be involved with one. It's a way to support your community and enrich your personal life. It's also a way to meet a lot of great prospects and build your reputation. Among the most prominent are:

Rotary. This civic club is responsible for the virtual eradication of polio around the world. It does a lot of work in third-world countries, but is also very visible in local communities. In my experience, it has the greatest number of business owners among the civic clubs.

Kiwanis. Usually a very socially active organization with a younger membership than Rotarians, it often includes the managers and vice presidents of major companies.

Jaycees. The youngest and liveliest of the civic clubs, it's the champion of social events and members often form relationships that last a lifetime. Members generally are 22 to 35 years old. As they age up, many Jaycees become Rotarians; their children often follow in their footsteps and become Jaycees.

The Halo Effect

One of the more coveted benefits of focusing your attention on a deeply connected group is the potential evolution of what's referred to as the "halo effect." This occurs when an advisor's involvement in a group's cause results in such a high profile that the audience segment embraces this person as one of their most esteemed and significant supporters. This relationship creates an almost instant preference.

Examples of groups that have deep dedication to a cause include cohesive ethnic groups (usually identified by dual traditions and an active dual foreign language); religious groups that are evangelical in their outreach for converts; and the gay and lesbian community.

Other groups with potential halo-effect opportunities are usually identified locally due to the nature of the community. Your community may have a tremendously active organization focused on minority- or women-owned businesses or on environmental or health issues.

By no means should you attempt to superficially infiltrate an organization solely for business purposes. Make sure your heart is involved. Also, if you're looking for a group that could potentially bestow the halo effect on you, and you find yourself questioning its cohesive strength or influence, it is probably not a legitimate candidate. Halo-effect organizations are easy to identify. They communicate regularly, have a passion for the "cause," and actively know one another.

Another significant source of client acquisition for many advisors comes from being a member of a leads group. Here is the story of the largest, not only in the United States but also in the world.

Business Network International

It is 7 a.m. You walk into a meeting room at a local restaurant. Professionals from a variety of businesses are gathered around the table, among them an accountant, human resource consultant and commercial realtor. After a few opening comments, each takes a turn describing their business and their perfect client.

Then the passing of referrals begins. Each member of the BNI (Business Network International) chapter now knows the perfect client you are looking for. Maybe the accountant is working with a small-business owner who needs to shelter more of his income from taxes. Or the HR person has a client who needs to pare employee benefits costs. The commercial realtor perhaps is working with a client who recently acquired a competitor and needs key-person insurance to cover his new partner.

Each passes you a name and number while offering to call and make the introduction for you. You must be dreaming! But it's not a dream. This scenario is actually happening in a great many places.

We are talking here about the largest referral group organization in the world. Shelli Howlett, executive director of BNI, started building chapters in Dallas in 1993. Thirty-eight chapters have been established in her area since then, and growth continues to accelerate.

Many financial advisors credit their involvement and the organization's spirit of giving as the most significant milestone for building their business success. Some members report earning as much as ninety-five percent of their total gross revenue as a result of BNI participation.

Most chapters have twenty-four members or more – one member per business category. Membership is by invitation only. Breakfast or luncheon meetings are held weekly, with each member giving a sixty-second business commercial telling what he or she does and describing the kind of prospect that would be a good referral. Then come the referrals – usually forty to sixty new names shared each time.

The structured meeting format and member accountability keep the focus where it should be – on helping members build their business. But other positive effects are reported as well, such as a heightened sense of community, confidence, self-esteem and even improved speaking skills. As one member noted, her sixty-second business commercial got better every week and transferred over to her ability to communicate better when asking for appointments and in her initial sales encounters.

BNI's upfront philosophy of "giving over getting" drives its success. "Referral groups provide a wealth of benefits to the members with current membership costing less than three hundred dollars per year, a token amount compared to the business generated and the market access gained," points out Shelli Howlett. The title of a book written about the organization by Ivan R. Misner says it all: *Givers Gain.*

IN SUMMARY, creating prospect attraction is the first step in your journey to becoming "a little bit famous." Here's how to get started:

• Set a time to get out from behind your desk for prospect building. Go to the library and locate your city's association directory. Find two or three organizations that you believe you could cultivate a genuine interest in and go visit. Evaluate if their membership is large enough and prosperous enough to support your financial objectives. Many organizations will have their memberships listed in the directory. All of them will give you a membership listing once you join, either in print or on CD.

• Start asking acquaintances for their e-mail addresses. Also ask where they work and who the owner is. Call and ask the receptionist for the e-mail addresses of the owner and the person in charge of benefits. Put these names in your database so you can begin a connection strategy.

• Determine to fill your prospect database with five hundred names within sixty days – one thousand is better. Get their names and personal information, including e-mail addresses, into your database.

• Consider joining a leads group. It's not hard to find a member you can ask to invite you as their guest. A single meeting should be adequate for you to come to a conclusion. There is no reason to delay this consideration. Find out now. For many, this has been a significant component to their success.

Please... Make ME a little bit FAMOUS

"Make ME a little bit FAMOUS" Notebook

My thoughts on how to apply this chapter's lessons to my business...

_____

_____

_____

_____

_____

_____

_____

_____

_____

_____

_____

_____

_____

_____

_____

_____

_____

_____

_____

_____

_____

_____

_____

_____

_____

_____

_____

"We repay in kind what another provides
for our personal benefit."

Robert E. Krumroy

Chapter Five

The PACC Model
• Step Two •

ACTIVATING EVENTS

Go public!

I'm sure you have heard those two words. But have you considered it your top priority for delivering YOU to your local market audience?

Creating a strategy to deliver highly visible, personal and unique experiential encounters throughout the year to your identified prospects and existing clients is imperative in today's competitive market. It is not an option if you want to attain high-level success and become a little bit famous.

There is no affection out there for sameness. We deplore it. And we shun salespeople who tell us they are better than the competition, basing their claim on a presentation of their product or planning-process superiority.

Creating affection requires giving, not getting. It is an emotional issue, not a product or a planning-process issue. It is not a single event. It is a cumulative process. And if you want the relationship to last, it is continuous.

Why are activating events so effective in creating preference or in getting prospects to enthusiastically agree to an appointment? The answer is simple. Here is your third rule for prospect attraction:

The Rule of Reciprocation

How it works.
We repay in kind what another provides for our personal benefit. Society teaches an implied agreement of reciprocation. We are taught from childhood to always say thank you. When invited to dinner, we take a bottle of wine or flowers. In return for good service, we tip. And we even have distaste for people who don't abide by this rule.

The lesson.
Extending yourself to prospects and clients in ways that have personal meaning creates a sense of obligation. It builds a sense of trust and safety, providing significant positive influence when asking for appointments. Activating events also give tangible personal value – not commercial value – to prospects and clients. This is measurably more valuable than persuasive phone skills or convincing arguments about products and benefits when trying to get in the door.

Inviting someone to a traditional seminar will not engage an act of reciprocation. Why has seminar attendance waned in recent years? Traditional seminars are largely viewed as self-serving, an attempt to sell something. People's opinion of traditional seminars has been negatively affected by their own numerous past experiences, not the least of which involves the time-share industry. Invitations to luncheons and free weekends incurred a painful sales encounter – one that most are determined never to repeat.

Seminars that are still effective are non-transactional seminars, often sponsored by sales-neutral organizations. For example, an evening with hors d'oeuvres (or a luncheon event) on "Preventing Identity Theft" has no transactional intent, especially if it is cosponsored by an organization such as a retirement home. If the event is fun and engaging, as high as sixty percent of those attending will fill out an evaluation form requesting additional information on such topics as avoiding taxation on 1099 interest income (a response that could lead to an annuity sale) or alternative investments that yield higher returns than their current bank CDs. The response is high at these types of events because nothing is expected in return. Even attendees who don't fill out a form are likely to graciously accept a phone call a day later and engage in a friendly conversation.

Some other examples that employ the rule of reciprocation:

• Taking digital photographs of every exhibitor's booth at a business trade show and sending an e-photo album to all the business owners

• Sending e-pictures of your church picnic to your entire congregation

• Sending e-pictures of a golf tournament to the association members

• Sponsoring a "Child ID Day" at a private school or retirement home for grandchildren

• Conducting morning CE credit sessions for CPAs – not in

public places such as a university or hotel but at their offices, providing doughnuts and making it a personal affair

Keep in mind that people with consistently high visibility usually have high likeability. They get a lot of invitations to social gatherings; they're asked to head organizations and serve on boards. They also do the most business in their field of endeavor. The professionals in your community who have the most visibility are also usually considered the top experts in their business sectors.

Is creating a strategy for delivering activating events to your market audience a dreaded chore? It shouldn't be! Not if you create a strategy around what you and your market audience appreciate.

On the following pages are some examples. Find one you could adopt or adapt… watch how the rule of reciprocation works… and get ready to become a little bit famous in your market.

The Trade Show Photo Album

Select at least two trade shows per year to attend, preferably in an organization your target audience attends or participates in. The Chamber's business expo or homebuilder's show might be examples. Purchase a ticket – not a booth. Take a digital camera and approach the people at each booth by handing them a business card and saying:

> *"My name is _____ and I specialize in working with small-business owners here in _____. However, I am not here to introduce my services or to ask for an appointment. That might be the highlight of your day – a financial guy not asking for an appointment?! (Wait for them to smile or chuckle.) No, I am here to take a picture so we can send you a trade show album that has photos of the fronts of all the booths. That way you can evaluate whether to adopt or adapt some other ideas to help increase your booth's attraction. My business clients always like this photo album and feel it has been really helpful over the years. I am not only doing it for my clients this year, but for all the owners participating in the show. Can I get your picture here in the booth?"*

Once you get an affirmative to your request, *which you always will,* ask for their business card and e-mail address, explaining you will be sending the album to them electronically. Tell them they can download the pictures or just view them occasionally to gather new ideas. Get the e-mail address of everyone in the booth. If the owner is not present, be sure to ask for that e-mail address. You will get it.

No later than seven days after the event, send the e-photo

album with the subject line: "Trade Show Photo Album." It will get opened. One week later, send an e-Financial Storyboard through www.e-Relationship.com. Use the same subject line: "Trade Show Photo Album." Start your message this way:

> "Hopefully you will remember that I sent you the Trade Show Photo Album last week. This is just one way that we support our business clients, helping them find ways to increase profits. We have had a lot of nice comments and words of appreciation. You might recall that I also promised to send you occasional financial briefs on areas that our business clients find valuable. Here is one of those briefs. See if you would like additional details. You can access the information below."

Think of other places where you could create an e-photo album – church picnic, vintage car show, civic club social, silent auction, charity wine tasting, Chamber member get-together, etc. – and follow up a week later with a financial message accentuating your professional business image.

The Digital Photo Appointment

It was Monday morning in Chicago. Brad, a successful financial advisor, had called my hotel the night before, wanting to take me flying in his private plane before the afternoon marketing workshop I was holding would begin. The calm weather, big billowy clouds lacing the blue sky, made it a perfect morning for the adventure.

We flew above the Chicago shoreline, taking in the towering buildings, the harbor boats, the luxury hotels and general scenery. Then we headed north. Fifteen minutes later, we came upon a home standing on ten acres of Lake Michigan shoreline. The home, no less than twenty-five thousand square feet, was magnificent. When Brad told me that the owner was a Chicago business tycoon, I asked if he had ever met the man – or better yet, whether he was a client. The answer was no. Brad had been referred to him more than once and had placed numerous calls to his office, but he had never been able to even initiate a phone conversation.

I reached for my digital camera and asked Brad to circle back and fly by the house as closely as he could. Four pictures later, we were heading back north, enjoying the rest of our sightseeing excursion.

Two hours later at Brad's office, we downloaded the photos. All of them turned out great. Placing a call to the businessman's office, Brad's assumption that he would reach an assistant was correct. Introducing himself, he explained that he was in the financial business but was not calling about business. He had been out flying in his plane and had snapped some digital photos of her boss's house. He thought "Mr. Big" would appreciate having them, and wanted to e-mail them to him.

Brad also offered to copy the assistant on the e-mail as a way to include her in the surprise. The e-mail addresses were given to him without hesitation. Brad asked the assistant to tell "Mr. Big" that the pictures would be arriving in a few minutes and to watch for them. Here was the e-mail message:

Dear (Name),

The other morning when I was flying my airplane (my hobby), I decided to take some aerial shots of your house. The pictures came out great. Though I took four pictures, you will note that only three are enclosed. The fourth picture was particularly neat, so I'm having it framed for you. I'm sure it will be a conversation piece no matter where you hang it!

I will call your office in a few minutes to schedule a time to deliver the framed picture to you. There is no catch! However, I would enjoy the opportunity to meet you and possibly grab lunch together. You can decide if that's okay after we talk. Meanwhile, I hope you enjoy the three pictures. You can access them here:
www.e-relationship.com/photo.

Sincerely,

Brad

Brad got his luncheon appointment. How could "Mr. Big" say no? (Remember the Rule of Reciprocation?) After six years of references and rebuffed appointment attempts, Mr. Big enthusiastically received Brad's phone call and scheduled a luncheon within the week to receive the framed photo of his home. Seven months later Brad sold Mr. Big a sizable insurance policy and took over management of two million dollars of his investment portfolio, a small portion of what could eventually develop but a great beginning.

Today, Brad is an avid digital photo-taker, often snapping shots of new homes, office buildings and even large yachts in the harbor – after getting the names of the owners first. He takes his camera when he flies, but he also keeps it handy in his briefcase to take pictures of new buildings and sidewalk office signage where the owner's name is displayed. He sends these photos before calling to introduce himself.

Brad has a new understanding that marketing is all about touching hearts and that people do business with those who make them feel special. Brad has become a little bit famous.

Group Luncheon Drawing

It's noon. Jim and thirteen guests have just sat down to a free lunch at a high-end Japanese restaurant.

Free?

Yes, absolutely free. A month earlier, Jim's business card was drawn from a fishbowl next to the restaurant's cash register – allowing him to bring up to fifteen guests to a complimentary meal.

The fishbowl is sponsored by a local financial planner, who calls Jim to assure him that no sales presentation will be made at the luncheon. The planner, Bill, will simply show up for a quick five minutes, introduce himself, thank them for coming, and hand out a small amount of information.

On the day of the luncheon, a hostess seats the group and takes their orders, explaining that everything is complimentary except for alcoholic beverages. Within minutes, Bill stops by the table and spends a few minutes conversing with them. He starts with a quick quiz: "Can anyone guess the value of investing a single dollar and allowing it to double each year for 20 years, assuming no tax?" Answers vary dramatically. The answer is then revealed: One million, forty-eight thousand dollars.

Bill then asks a second question: "Can someone guess the value if it is taxed at just 28 percent?" This draws a flurry of guesses. He quickly distributes an illustration showing the value is only fifty-one thousand dollars.

The startled looks and comments say it all. He emphasizes that most people don't take financial planning seriously enough. "They buy an occasional insurance policy, invest money in their company's 401k plan, and save a little extra for vacations and future expenditures. But they don't have well-coordinated financial plans, at least not ones that are regularly monitored and measured as to performance."

Before departing, Bill distributes simple registration forms, explaining that he needs them to be completed for his tax records.

Along with space for basic information, the registration form includes fifteen boxes that guests can check if they would like to receive information about a variety of financial issues, such as current wealth strategies, methods for reducing taxes, children's college funds, etc.

It's worth noting that every one of the luncheon guests checks at least one box, giving Bill future opportunities to call. Additionally noteworthy is that Jim, who won the free lunch, already has provided Bill with a referral (a colleague at work who is retiring and needs to move his 401k account).

This scenario is being played out across the country every day. Some financial advisors also report success in having mutual fund companies share the expense of the lunch – in return for having their products promoted when purchases are made. Sales results determine how long the cost-share arrangement will last.

This might sound too good to be true, but it definitely is not. Some advisors have used this strategy with great success for many years, often meeting individuals at lunch who had attended earlier lunches with another guest.

This is all in the advisor's favor. Repetition. Being seen over and over. Building trust. Feeling a need to respond. It's a perfect example of the Rule of Reciprocation (returning in kind when a personal benefit is extended to us).

Bill sponsors the free lunch twice a month. He likes the results – and what's not to like? After all, it's making him become a little bit famous.

$1 DOUBLES EVERY YEAR AT 0% TAX
versus
$1 DOUBLES EVERY YEAR AT 28% TAX

End of Year	Tax Deferred-0% Tax	Taxable-28% tax
1	$2	$1.72
2	$4	$3
3	$8	$5
10	$1,024	$227
15	$32,726	$3,411
18	$262,144	$17,358
20	$1,048,576	$51,353

Note:
Starting in year 2 numbers have been rounded to the nearest dollar.

The Appreciation Ambassador Doughnut Giveaway

Approach your Chamber of Commerce and ask to be an appreciation ambassador to companies that have been members for at least five years. If the position doesn't exist, ask the Chamber to create it and give assurances that you will be happy to carry out the duties.

Bingo! You will be the Chamber's only appreciation ambassador to be working with member companies.

Now, select a member business you want to meet and call on behalf of the Chamber. Set a time when you can drop by with doughnuts (a dozen or two) for their employees or office staff. Tell them you simply want to say thanks for their years of Chamber membership and present them with a packet of information on the current ways the organization is assisting business growth in the community.

Take a new-member package and review all the support, opportunities and upcoming Chamber meetings. While there, emphasize that being an appreciation ambassador is just your way of adding value to the community and that it fits with your profession of working exclusively with businesses. Take a minute and discuss what you do – but *don't oversell.*

Ask if you can set a time to grab lunch in the next week. During that luncheon provide them with some samples of the type of work you do for businesses similar to theirs. Samples could illustrate how you help others save on taxes and increase after-tax wealth. Do this at least once a week; twice is better.

It is a guaranteed ninety percent appointment getter and positions you on a very favorable basis. Not only will the

Chamber president become your number-one ally, but you can always ask their opinion of a certain business, how strong their personal relationship is with the owner, and whether it would be okay to tell the business owner the president suggested you call on them. Not only will you gain a lot of business, but you also get into businesses you would have spent years trying to cultivate.

The doughnut cost? Go to a local doughnut place and explain that you are an ambassador for the Chamber of Commerce. Explain how your job is to identify an established Chamber member business to visit each week. Ask them to become the official doughnut provider for this endeavor – contributing the doughnuts and also a dollar-off coupon for every employee purchasing a dozen on their own in the next month. Every financial professional involved in this idea has had a doughnut company say yes.

The New Chamber Member
Doughnut Giveaway

This is an abbreviated variation on the previous idea. It is less selective as to whom you get to meet, but it will put you in front of new businesses that are joining the Chamber of Commerce for the first time.

Volunteer to be a new-member ambassador with your local Chamber. There will be a number of other ambassadors already in the organization, but volunteers are always welcome. All Chambers have this program.

Volunteer not only for such events as ribbon cuttings, but add a unique twist to the Chamber's ambassador program by offering to personally deliver new-member packets along with a dozen doughnuts each week. No one is going to be upset by your bringing doughnuts and welcoming their new business into the community. And most of them will be happy to schedule lunch with you the next week in exchange for your kindness.

Does it work? Yes! Dozens of advisors do it now and report **great** success and friendly welcomes. It will quickly become the fun highlight of your week.

The Golf Tournament Surprise

Organizations of all stripes sponsor annual golf tournaments to benefit charities – the Homebuilder's Association, the country club's member-guest tournament, the Chamber of Commerce, the Merchants Association, the American Heart and Lung Association, the Cancer Association, and most manufacturing associations. Don't forget your church, synagogue and civic club, as well as service companies such as Enterprise Rent-A-Car, which extends invitations to its corporate business clients. Many of these organizations are full of business owners and affluent individuals, prospects you would like to reach. Through a simple phone call to local private and public golf clubs, the golf pro (who is in charge of helping find sponsors) will enthusiastically tell you who is holding these events and how much it will cost to sponsor a hole (usually one hundred to one hundred fifty dollars).

Do not sign up to play in the tournament! Instead, ask to sponsor the watering hole. That's the hole that supplies free beer and soft drinks to the golfers. Tell them you will take a digital photo of each foursome, conduct a longest-drive marshmallow contest, and send an e-photo album to all the golfers thanking them for participating. You might also announce the winners and how much money was raised for charity due to their participation.

The following year, volunteer to send e-invitations to participants on behalf of the cause or provide the organization with the e-mail addresses. Make sure you have a yellow legal pad (or index cards) for golfers to write down their names and e-mail addresses. If you use pre-printed cards, you can ask for company name, birth date, financial areas of interest, and any other information you want.

Want to be exceptionally memorable? Tell the golfers that you are sponsoring the "win-a-car" hole. No hole-in-one requirement: just whoever wins the longest marshmallow drive contest wins the car. Have three marshmallows for each golfer. They will all be laughing and asking for multiple marshmallows since this is such a novelty.

As far as the car prize goes… they will all accuse you of lying, but have fun and insist that it is absolutely true. Have a matchbox car hidden in your pocket – they only cost about eighty-nine cents apiece – and at the conclusion of your contest, pull it out and present it to the winner. Take another picture of the golfer (or foursome) with the prize in hand. They will love it, and you will be remembered at the end of the day as the most fun hole anyone visited.

The matchbox car will become an icon during the tournament. Look distinct. Be different! And remember that exceptional difference is what pays off the most!

In making your initial contact with a golf course, here is the type of dialogue that should occur:

> As part of my annual plans for promoting myself with the community, I try to sponsor a hole in a number of golf tournaments in order to meet new people and see old friends in an atmosphere where everyone is having fun. When I sponsor a hole, I always take pictures of all the foursomes and then send each person a photo of the tournament along with final results – both of the scoring, the winning golfers and the amount of money raised.
>
> I also get e-mail addresses so we can send the photo album to every participant – plus I will provide a copy of the e-mail database to your organization so you can invite the

players back next year. We find that taking pictures always works best at the watering hole, where the foursomes seem to get very social. If play gets backed up, we usually have a marshmallow-driving contest (longest drive) at our hole and give out prizes to the winner.

The teeing of marshmallows is always a smile-inducing moment. In other words, we try to make our hole a really memorable event. Can you tell me if the watering hole would be a possibility?

Email the photo album to participants within three days after the tournament. Follow up five days later by sending them an e-Financial Storyboard. You will get a lot of favorable responses and leads.

Join the HR Association

Building high-level visibility and professional recognition in your local market requires that you become consistently recognized by the same prospects – prospects who are candidates for your area of business focus.

Most sales people utilize no strategy that builds constant knowledge of their business expertise through making relevant connections and continuously drawing prospects closer to them. Creating prospect attraction is an ongoing courting process. Creating easy approachability requires delivering yourself (not your product) frequently to your market audience. Without consistent visibility, you have little chance of building personal likeability or accentuating your professional business image, especially to high-level prospects.

Join an association full of business owners, or at least people who have access to decision makers, and get involved. Organizations that fit this description may be the Rotary Club, Kiwanis, manufacturing associations or HR associations.

A major focus of HR associations is employee benefits – keeping plans effective but also affordable. Human resource professionals in most companies have the ability to deliver you into their business and to the owner. Why not get involved in their association?

Become an ally. Bank executives join and are involved for this very reason – building relationships that turn into business opportunities. Have lunch once a month with association members. Volunteer to create an e-photo album for their golf tournament or social function, such as a holiday luncheon.

Request a ghostwritten article from your primary financial company and submit it to their executive director for inclusion in their association newsletter.

Put all of the members in your database and e-mail an occasional financial briefing to them. Get their birth dates and send an e-birthday card as well as a variety of e-holiday cards throughout the year. Build personal affection in a defined market with consistent contact and watch your business grow.

The CPA Lunch and Bagel Connection

CPAs can lead you into a lot of business. But heightening their awareness of you, while building trust and likeability, requires more than an occasional lunch or a quick visit when seeing each other in the community. Building meaningful awareness and preference is a process that takes time and strategy.

Create a list of CPAs (at least twenty-five) with whom you would like to build a relationship. Then, on their busiest days of the year – April 14 (the day before tax-filing deadline), August 15 (first-extension date), and October 15 (last-extension date) – take box lunches to their offices.

A turkey and havarti croissant, cookie, chips and an apple cost about five dollars. Vary the menu for August by taking a bagel platter; in October, take a cookie, doughnut or sausage biscuit tray. These encounters will surprise and delight them, which is always the first element of getting attention.

Don't have a catering company deliver the food. Do it personally. Clear your schedule for April 15 so you can receive the numerous thank-you calls. Don't expect a huge onslaught of business after that first endeavor (though this has happened). Be patient. You can expect some serious referrals after doing this consistently for a year and the CPAs realize you are a trusted ally. Paperclip your business card to a pre-printed note and insert it into each lunch carton. Here's an example of what to say in the note:

Dear CPA,

We both know that today is a very taxing day for the average citizen in America. I also know that today's workload makes it a very taxing day for you – which may

*make it difficult for you to get out to lunch or even dinner.
I hope that this snack pack helps in that regard. Consider
it a small appreciation for your work and contributions to
my clients (many of whom you and I share, though we
have never discussed that).*

*Many of my clients are very appreciative of their CPAs,
often commenting about the trust and prudent advice they
receive. Again, my thanks for the value that you deliver. It
makes a difference. If I can ever provide information on
insurance, investments or employee benefit packages,
please feel free to ask. It is always a pleasure hearing from
my CPA friends and clients.*

Sincerely,
(name)
(phone number)

Remember: Creating a lasting local market presence, one that
outclasses the competition, requires consistency. One-time
events don't build big results. It's what you do consistently
that eventually places you – and keeps you – at the front of
people's minds and builds big results. Advisors who deliver
lunches on April 14, follow up with bagels on August 15, and
maybe a biscuit tray on October 15 will eventually see their
efforts pay off. Many report major sales increases from CPA
referrals who call them. Great alliance relationships evolve by
initiating touch-points that create "linkage to the heart" and
differentiate you from the competition.

Wondering what to say if you decide to do the follow-up
bagel delivery on August 15? Try this:

Dear CPA,

August 15 is always a big day in the life of a CPA – I know that today's workload can consume about every minute of your available time. How do I know? A lot of my financial work includes working with CPAs, in coordination with my clients. (It's how I prefer to work, especially with my more affluent clients.)

Why these bagels? Hopefully they will again say "thanks" for the value you give to my clients, many of whom we unknowingly share. If I can ever provide you with information about insurance, insurance funding techniques, qualified plans or other financial issues, please give me a call. It is always good hearing from my CPA friends. Enjoy the bagels. Maybe someday soon we can grab lunch.

Branding YOU as distinctly different – and preferred by CPAs – requires more than just an occasional seminar, lunch or contact initiative. It requires multiple and consistent connection, different from what the competition delivers. Be different! Be consistent! Stay visible! The eventual results will be far greater than the effort exerted.

Conducting CPA CE Seminars

Thirty-six percent of accountants made referrals of affluent clients to life insurance professionals in the last year, according to Russ Prince and Karen File, authors of the book *Marketing Through Advisors*. There is, however, a catch.

In order for you to effectively position yourself to win over advisors, you will need to become an expert at creating awareness about yourself, your practice and the services you provide. In their interviews with CPAs, Prince and File said they found that most advisors (nearly ninety-one percent) make the mistake of looking for a referral handout every time they are with their CPA. CPAs are unanimously unappreciative of this (zero percent) and they do not regard it as an effective way to build the relationship. The goal should be to provide value.

Display your expertise by giving private, quarterly CE seminars – at their firm, not at an offsite location. Conducting CE seminars at colleges or libraries for the entire CPA community minimizes your ability to interact one-on-one; assures that no one will ask questions; and they certainly won't ask about a personal client. However, this will occur when the CE seminar is held in the privacy of their own offices.

Print a yearly index card listing the subjects of your quarterly CE seminars. Get on your CPA's quarterly schedule for four sessions throughout the year (7 a.m. to 9 a.m. is best). Offer to bring doughnuts and ask them to provide coffee. Maintain a constant connection, asking how you can help with their needs. Be patient and don't ask for referrals. When they consider you an ally and you have attained preference, you will be rewarded often.

Just remember that this is a long-term project. Be consistent in providing CE opportunities in their office and patient in giving the process adequate time to yield results.

Brilliant Strategies and Fatal Blunders

Want to build an ally relationship with business owners, where they consider you a trusted partner and a little bit famous? After this event, it will be easy to get in to see a business owner.

My book, *Brilliant Strategies and Fatal Blunders: How Small Business Owners Survive and Thrive in an Overcrowded Market* is used at numerous universities. It is also a video seminar that targets the business owner who wants to establish a greater competitive advantage, establish market dominance, increase profits and build deeper client loyalty. This seminar is frequently co-sponsored by local Chambers of Commerce, national small-business incubation centers, civic clubs, merchant associations, law firms and CPA firms that wish to provide value-added benefits for their clients.

The video seminar directs how you facilitate the event: welcoming the audience, introducing the seminar, playing three video sections, and directions for facilitating two ten-minute group discussions. Everything is scripted for your use; even the invitations are prewritten for you or the organization to send out and attract the audience.

The seminar can be run in one ninety-minute setting or in two settings. After it is completed, call attendees within the week, ask how they enjoyed the event, and offer to bring them a copy of the book – your gift to them for attending the seminar. You can expect one hundred percent acceptance of your appointment requests and an easy opening to discuss how you work with business owners.

For more information about the seminar package, call (800) 851.8169.

The International Adoption Evening

Scott and Mary had already adopted two Asian girls. They knew the ropes, so to speak. They had gone through the emotional process as a couple: the paperwork, the adoption process, the approval waiting period, the overseas trip, the acclamation period in a foreign country, and then the long flight back home with their infant daughter. Their hearts were both committed. The adoption agency often referred people who were considering international adoption to them.

Mary decided that connecting her passion for international adoption with her financial prospects was a natural. She was right. It automatically connected her with those who shared a deep social commonality.

Each quarter Mary and Scott work with the adoption agency to sponsor an evening for potential adoptive parents, rotating the gathering among several churches. Their reputation in the organization has soared, but two events have really played a major role in Mary's business attraction and sales success. Every summer, they sponsor a picnic for parents who have adopted an international child. Every Christmas, they sponsor a holiday evening just for the parents, always encouraging them to bring pictures to share.

These two events have positioned them as almost-celebrities within their international adoption community. They have become regarded as people who give of themselves in such a big way that you can't help but want to know them, conclude that you like them, and certainly feel that you trust them. Those are the three elements that must precede most people's consideration before accepting an interview with you, much less conducting business. Know me. Like me. Trust me.

Think about how a passion you have for something could provide a direct link to your prospect attraction and success. Are you overly concerned that promoting your business reputation would infringe on a shared commonality? That is a groundless concern. People with a shared commonality would be very open to doing business with you if they had a greater awareness and deeper understanding of what you do.

Too often, people who share a natural connection with advisors have very little idea of what they do. Most advisors have no strategy for establishing, accentuating and maintaining their business awareness to this audience.

Organizations like Promise Keepers, Catholic Men's Club and the Jewish Federation are all examples. Even a civic club membership is an easy way to initiate a biannual social event. How about inviting individuals you work alongside at Habitat for Humanity, volunteer with at Hospice, or serve with on the United Arts Council. Isn't there some connection you have that, if strategized effectively, could provide an easy bridge for business? The people with whom you already share a social connection are waiting. You could easily become their advisor of choice with a frequent connection strategy and a personal touch.

The Volunteer Firefighter
Annual Recognition Event

In Debbie's little community of five thousand, everyone knows everyone. Her objective was to build personal appreciation, separate herself from the competition and create heightened awareness, all of which could play a major role in helping her meet her second-year goals as a financial advisor.

In a conversation, she was asked to think about what her community rallied around. Her response: volunteer firefighters. The volunteers were all well known, tremendously appreciated and nearly always mentioned in the local newspaper when something significant happened. She decided to approach the mayor about holding an annual appreciation dinner for them.

Not only was the mayor all for the idea, but he also proclaimed Volunteer Firefighter Appreciation Day and suggested that the mayors of two adjoining towns be approached and given the same opportunity. He made a call to those mayors, suggesting they talk to Debbie when she called and hear her plans for this annual event. During those discussions with the mayors, it was further suggested that the local state representative be invited and included in the program. The legislator was delighted to participate and also decided to issue a proclamation.

Debbie approached the fire chief, and the town meeting hall was reserved for free. A catering company was willing to contribute the chicken, slaw, baked beans, iced tea and banana pudding at cost, allowing all proceeds of the ticket sales to benefit the fire department. Local business owners were solicited for door prizes, and more than sixty contributions were made, including gas grills, pots and pans, gift certificates, nursery plants, lamps, oil changes, electrical and plumbing work, power-washing, etc. Debbie invited a mutual fund company to participate and to pick up the cost of the food (which was minimal).

Tickets were sold by every business that gave door prizes, plus by the Kiwanis Club and at the county courthouse and fire department. The newspaper gave free advertising. The high school provided a jazz band.

The evening began with Debbie welcoming everyone and introducing the mayors to read their proclamations. The state legislator's proclamation was last. He talked about the contribution of the firefighters and thanked them for their sacrifice of time and sense of duty. He also thanked Debbie for making the event possible.

Debbie then introduced the mutual fund manager to recognize him for contributing money for the food and for supporting the community even though his business wasn't located there. Asked to say a few words, he gave Debbie the kind of advertising money can't buy, saying something like:

> "I feel honored to be a part of this worthy cause that Debbie has championed. If you don't know Debbie, you should. If we could clone her, we would. Her commitment to your community is no different from what we've observed in her dealings with her clients. She is professional. She is honorable. She has a deep dedication to doing what is right, to putting the client first. Hopefully, you have all become her clients. (Ha-ha). I can't imagine anyone I would rather have handle my investments and insurance than her. Please join me in a round of applause for the lady who made this happen, one of the most giving people I have ever had the privilege of working with."

After those quick comments, Debbie and the state legislator took over the fun part of the program, awarding the sixty door prizes. There was no financial speech, no brochures, no product or service pitch. The program was about honoring the firefighters and giving out door prizes.

Did it pay off with new business? Debbie applied for Million Dollar Round Table membership that year, with commissions exceeding seventy thousand dollars. The firefighter appreciation dinner has become a yearly event, and Debbie is still its master of ceremonies. She has become a little bit famous.

The Annual Child ID Event

Child safety is one of the primary concerns of parents today. According to the National Center for Missing and Exploited Children (NCMEC), as many as one million children are reported missing every year. Hosting a child-identification event gives you a chance to connect with the community, support a worthy cause, build personal ties with potential clients and become a little bit famous. These events are an easy, smart way to network and enhance your professional reputation in selected markets.

The NCMEC and Polaroid Corporation developed the Project KidCare ID program a dozen years ago. At KidCare events, each child is provided a personal safety document that includes a current photograph. The photos are taken by uniformed police officers, who also handle all of the paperwork for the day at no cost to you.

Your job? Find an organization that wants to sponsor the event annually, help develop a strategy for publicizing it to parents, and be present on the day of the event to greet families, shake hands and take digital photos of the whole thing. This program is enthusiastically received when presented at public and private schools, day care centers, retirement homes (inviting grandchildren), churches, temples and synagogues.

More information about the KidCare Project is available at Polaroid's Web site, www.polaroid.com (type "kidcare" in the search box). You can order a planning kit at the site, including news releases, announcement flyers, radio scripts and an agenda for the event. Many cities now provide the individual ID kits for free. If you do need to purchase them, consider letting your local PTA use the event as a fundraiser, sending flyers to parents, getting permission from them to photograph their children (see permission slip format on following page), and requesting a five-dollar contribution. Parents who cannot afford the five dollars should be included in the event at no charge. If kits are ordered, Polaroid will customize them with your name, company name, address and phone number.

Now that you have built a name-specific database, established your presence, given value by providing community children with identification tags – including photo and fingerprinting – it is pretty simple to initiate a consistent communication program to continue to build your awareness with parents. After all, they already know and appreciate you. You gave them value without expecting anything in return – and this never goes unnoticed. Not only will your sales soar, but so will your confidence when you have a thousand names of parents who will welcome hearing from you.

Child ID Event Permission Slip

Thank you for letting (your business name) provide you with a photo ID and documented information about your child. You have just taken an important step in protecting them. Be sure to keep your KidCare photo ID packet in a safe and easy-to-remember place.

I grant permission for my child (or grandchild) to participate in Child ID Day, sponsored by (your business name), KidCare and the local police department. Please send me information on next year's Child ID event. You may also send me periodic information on financial subjects such as college funding, reducing taxes and investment tips. I understand that my personal information will not be shared with any other party and that I can elect out of receiving future information at any time.

Name of Child _____

Parent or Attending Adult (Print)_____

Signature _____

E-mail Address _____

Address _____

Phone _____

The Football Game-Ball Giveaway

Sarah is a traditional multi-line insurance agent living in a rural community of four thousand. When strategizing how to increase her public visibility, she gave much thought to what enjoyed high recognition in her little town. The answer: The local high school football team. People flocked to the school's Friday night games and closely followed the team's fortunes in the weekly newspaper.

Sarah approached the high school, offering to purchase a game ball to be signed by the team and given away at every home game during the season. Accompanied by the team's most-valuable player during the first half, Sarah took the field at halftime to pull a winning admission ticket from a hat and present the lucky fan with the ball as a photographer captured the moment for the local newspaper. During homecoming a game program was signed on a certain page by the team captain, and the fan holding that program was presented with the ball.

In addition, Sarah got the football coach to agree to a photo-op session after a couple of the games, inviting the young children of fans to have their pictures taken with the players. She sends those photos (both print and electronic versions) to the parents.

Sarah has been involved in this event for three years and is a qualifying member of the Million Dollar Round Table. She has become a little bit famous.

The Recreational Photo Event

Nothing will make a parent appreciate you more than when you do something for their child.

This idea is a natural if you have a son or daughter of your own on a recreational team. Take a digital camera to the next game and snap pictures of each child while in play. Their parents will be more than happy to give you an e-mail address so you can send them the photo. From that point forward, it is pretty easy to begin a conversation about what you do and to call shortly thereafter to request an appointment. (Remember the Rule of Reciprocation.) Implement an e-mail strategy to continue sending them financial storyboards, holiday cards, birthday cards and checklists – all of which will continue to build your professional business image and increase your personal likeability.

An agent in Ohio who loves baseball became a legend using this strategy. Always involved in Little League, he approached the person in charge of the city's league and offered to go to each team and take action photos of every player. The league loved the idea and accepted enthusiastically.

According to the agent, more than five hundred parents approached him during the second season of this event to say thanks for the previous year's photos. He gets constant recognition throughout the year in the community and now has more than two thousand parents in his database. Appointments have never been easier to attain, and his business has soared. He has become a little bit famous.

The Annual Recreational Coaches Event

If you help coach a youth sport, approach the organization's executive director about co-sponsoring an annual appreciation event for coaches. Suggest buying out a performance (comedy theme is best) at a small local live theater (capacity, one to two hundred) and invite coaches and their spouses/guests to a special evening just for them.

The theater will reduce the rates dramatically, especially if the executive director contacts them. Arrange for a local wine merchant to sponsor a tasting at intermission. Ask the theater for a special introduction before the performance (or allow you to do it) to recognize and thank the coaches for their contribution and acknowledge that this event was due to your personal appreciation of what coaches add to the lives of the children they influence.

Tell the executive director you would be glad to design and send e-invitations and follow up with phone calls in order to increase attendance. Even those who don't attend will notice your efforts and appreciate your gesture and uniqueness. Contact the local newspaper to cover the event as a news story. Keep the names of the coaches on file and include them in your informational e-mailings and e-cards (eight to twelve times a year) and invite them to other events you conduct throughout the year.

Your high profile will quickly turn into welcome access, making coaches a prospect market you will dominate in your community. After all, you just became a little bit famous.

The Golf Course Alliance

The average golfer plays at more than one course, and usually the reason is not because he or she gave that choice a lot of thought. Maybe a golfing buddy suggested it. Or maybe a course just happened to come to mind. Most people make choices based on a product that happens to be on their mind at the time. (That's why Coca-Cola and McDonald's have among the largest advertising budgets in America.)

The more often a product is used and a consumer's mind is engaged, the more that advertising makes sense. Even though golfing is not a daily purchase for most, a course that becomes recognized as uniquely different from the competition will see an increase in business and revenue.

Since financial issues are among Americans' biggest concerns, approach a golf course owner about co-sponsoring a financial-and-golf e-newsletter. (This idea works best if you personally frequent a public or semi-private golf course.) The newsletter would be sent out to the course's customers at least four times a year through your e-mail system (www.e-relationship.com). You offer to provide the newsletter, prominently display their name along with yours, and include a caption that reads:

A Financial and Golf Newsletter
Provided by XYZ Golf Course
Finances and golf swings both require concentration.
We don't want you to miss a stroke.

The second part of the offer is to sponsor an annual or biannual event at the course's clubhouse, such as the "XYZ

Golf Course Golf Equipment Show, Financial Tips, Cigar Evening, Beer Tasting and Cookout."

A golf equipment vendor and cigar merchant will gladly split the cost of the cookout. Offer to coordinate the mailing and facilitate the event. This simple idea is more effective and better promotion than any single advertisement and is normally less expensive than one display ad in the local newspaper. Plus, it will create a reputation for being different and unique, increasing mind-share.

Suggest that the golf course try this idea for one year and then measure the results. Everyone will be pleased, and you will connect in a very meaningful way with prospects you have never met.

The Property & Casualty Alliance

Most P&C firms are resistant to opening their entire files to a financial advisor without any control. On the other hand, it is unrealistic for the average firm to think that clients will take the initiative and contact them when they're ready for a buy-sell, deferred compensation plan, age-weighted profit-sharing plan, or even a simple mutual fund or financial plan. It simply won't happen.

Offer to help them create greater brand appeal and higher-level familiarity with their clientele through a regular e-newsletter that provides educational information, not product solicitation. Be sure to have a sample joint e-newsletter to show them. You can request one from info@identitybrand-ing.com.

You need to be responsible for the e-newsletter mailing, but control of replies and client contacts should be offered to the P&C firm. To provide maximum benefit for both of you, the newsletter or financial brief must provide an easy way for readers to request more information. Allow reader responses to go directly back to the firm with a copy to you. The firm can then review the responses and decide how much control they want to maintain, such as requesting that a client meeting be scheduled jointly or held in their office. Once the relationship develops, you will see more authority delegated to you as confidence builds that you have their best interest at heart and not your own pocketbook.

Remember that your job in the relationship should be viewed as helping to develop the brand reputation of the P&C firm, not your own. Gaining more clients for yourself will happen as a result of focusing on giving rather than getting. You will create an alliance that is incredibly valuable to both parties.

The Association New Member Welcome

Having decided that homebuilder's would be his primary focus for business, Brad, an insurance agent in the Midwest, joined the local homebuilder association. He subsequently learned that two competing insurance professionals were already involved in the group, but he also became aware that neither of them had done anything to become dominant. Brad decided to strategize a way to "stand out" and came up with this idea.

He approached the executive director and asked if he could sponsor a quarterly get-acquainted/networking event for new members and members of less than two years. The invitees were allowed to bring two guests.

Brad said he would provide food and beer as part of the event. He approached a bank (one that loaned a lot of money to the building trades) and asked it to donate the food. He asked a beverage wholesaler to sponsor the beer. Both were delighted to have the exposure, and Brad felt this would be a great opportunity to make an impression on potential business clients.

The only involvement that Brad wanted was to welcome the attendees, which would naturally position him as the financial advisor who specialized working within the construction industry. He would introduce the bank and the beer sponsor and then explain the ground rules: Everyone was instructed that their job during the get-together was to introduce themselves to at least two members they did not know, ask questions about what they specialized in, and then try to assist them with finding a way to further their business – whether giving them a referral or the name of someone who would be beneficial for them to connect with. He encourages each individual to call the referral the next day, clearing the way for a favorable reception when the new member calls. In other words, the purpose of the encounter was to give, not get. Enthusiasm for this event was overwhelming. (Robert Littell, author of, *The Heart and Art of NetWeaving,* writes in extensive detail about this networking process)

Brad collects names, addresses and e-mails from all of the attendees and includes them in the financial newsletter he sends out eight times a year. He also invites them to investment events and eventually calls on all of them for a lunch meeting.

Brad's business has increased significantly. He has virtually an open door to any of the eight hundred builders and service providers in the local construction industry. He no longer worries about who the competition is. He has become the dominant financial advisor in the homebuilder's association. After all, Brad has become a little bit famous.

The Five Wishes Event

Traditional seminars don't pull attendance like they once did. There's a multitude of reasons for this: skepticism, worn-out subjects, greater consumer awareness, too little time, the perception that seminars are a camouflage for selling – similar to time-share presentations. However, being able to influence a number of people at once is still a wise use of your time, if you can figure out how to accomplish the objective.

One type of seminar that continues to attract people is the third-party seminar, which is an event sponsored by service or nonprofit organizations such as hospitals, civic groups and retirement homes. If the subject matter addresses pertinent social issues that everyone is talking about – such as identity theft or living wills – you're practically guaranteed an audience.

The "Your Life, Your Wishes" seminar fits this description. It's built around "The Five Wishes" health power-of-attorney document put out by the Aging with Dignity Foundation of Tampa, Florida. Most hospitals give this document to new, incoming patients.

Numerous hospital marketing departments run this seminar two or three times a year, with free public service ads placed prominently in newspapers and on radio. The hospitals also send invitations to their own prospect mailing lists – often residents who live in close proximity to the facility. They see these events as a way to get local people to visit their hospital – assuring future business.

Assure a hospital of future business? Yes! They want to make sure they are regarded as the hospital of choice. Providing an event that is educational and free and has no obligation attached to it helps people come to the conclusion that they like you and trust you. Sound familiar?

What makes this seminar so attractive to being facilitated by a financial professional is the percentage of attendees who indicate on the evaluation form their willingness to be contacted in the future about financial issues. These financial issues might be worded thusly:

- Please provide information on ways to avoid taxation on 1099 forms.
- Please provide information on alternative investments that yield higher returns than my current bank CD.

These requests for information often run as high as eighty percent. Why? Because when an event is fun and meaningful and nothing is expected in return, you increase your likeability, appreciation and, most important, trust. And that, by itself, engenders a feeling of obligation on the part of the attendee.

If you want to conduct seminars, consider finding a non-selling third party that will mutually benefit from the increased exposure. It shouldn't be a one-time event. Set a schedule and offer it at least twice a year so that you gain local distinction as the expert. Consistency is the foundation of brand recognition – becoming the expert in the field.

The "Your Life, Your Wishes" seminar, available through Identity Branding, includes:

- A professional PowerPoint presentation customized with your name on the presentation.
- A detailed presentation guide that will make you look like a true expert.

- A dozen "Five Wishes" documents for participants. (Additional copies can be purchased for one dollar each.)
- A professionally designed tri-fold brochure and evaluation form.
- An automated LCD video trivia quiz that runs on the screen while attendees are filling the room (to help break the ice).

This is a great seminar to introduce to hospital marketing departments, retirement homes, senior centers, churches, etc. For more information or to order, call Identity Branding at (800) 851.8169.

The Tomato Giveaway

High-level attraction in your local market requires creating what I call unique RPMs (Remarkable Positive Memories) with a pinpointed audience. These emotional contacts build "linkage to the heart." They make the prospect smile. And when people smile, they are buying you.

Consider Mark, an agent who specializes in working with seniors. He has two hundred thirty clients, but equally important are the eleven hundred prospects for which he has names, addresses and e-mail information.

How did he get them?

Mark loves to garden and often finds himself at the farmer's market. He noticed one day that the early morning crowd seemed older than the midday crowd. With this in mind, he decided to rent a stall, arrive extra early and purchase one hundred pounds of tomatoes (at approximately seventy-five cents a pound). He put up a sign that read "Senior Citizens – One FREE Pound of Tomatoes. Ask For Details."

The details were that he would give away a pound of tomatoes in exchange for one e-mail address. He gave away all of the tomatoes, and the next week he purchased two hundred pounds of tomatoes and put up the same sign. A month later, Mark had amassed more than six hundred e-mail addresses and, incidentally, had made more than ten thousand dollars in annuity sales.

Selling to everyone was never his intention. He wanted the e-mail addresses so he could send them e-greeting cards (birthday, anniversary, holiday, etc.), his annual e-financial checklist and quarterly e-Financial Storyboards. Over the course of a year, about fifteen percent of these prospects responded with thank-you notes or requests to call them. A tremendous number became clients.

Mark understands the importance of creating a consistent and likable connection strategy. It's the key to opening doors.

Tomatoes may or may not be your thing, but if you work in the senior market, strategize how to connect with these people in a fun and engaging way while building your database and becoming a little bit famous.

The Health Store Alliance

Business owners who are great marketers embrace alliances with strategic partners. One of the most striking examples is that of Barnes & Noble and Starbucks. Someone had the foresight to recognize that if Starbucks customers could spend three dollars and fifty cents for a cup of coffee, they probably could afford to buy books; and if Barnes & Noble customers could afford expensive books, they would also be willing to buy expensive coffee.

On a much smaller scale, Gary Bargebuhr, a certified financial planner, and Health Nuts, a store in Greensboro, North Carolina, illustrate as well the success to be gained from alliance marketing.

Bargebuhr graduated from the New York Institute of Technology with a degree in business and economics in 1985 and joined a financial services company, focusing primarily on insurance and secondarily on mutual fund sales. By 1990, his passion for focusing on the investment side was too great to ignore. He made a career change and joined Shearson Lehman Hutton (which later became Salomon Smith Barney) as an investment brokerage representative.

By 2000, Bargebuhr had worked his way to the top twenty-five percent of brokerage representatives in his firm. He was out-producing other brokers with far more years of experience. Gary looked at his career differently. He focused not just on selling, but on intentionally developing a personal business image, a strong local identity, by creating a specific strategy to capture not just business but more of his clients' attention and loyalty.

The famous line from the movie *Field of Dreams* – "If you

build it, they will come" – rings in his head like it was said to him personally. Maybe that was the cause of his initial thinking about how to build deeper attraction in his community. It certainly was influential on Gary's strategy to align with other organizations and companies that could equally benefit from connecting with their customers more frequently.

Health Nuts principals Greg Eason and Bobby Layne likewise often pondered how to create and maintain a differentiation in their business. They invested extra time talking with their clients, answering questions and learning about their products in depth. They saw great marketing in terms of having the courage to trial-test new ideas and to adapt and change.

To Gary Bargebuhr, Health Nuts customers seemed a direct parallel to his financial clients. The great majority who shopped at the store cared about their long-term health; they weren't looking for a quick elixir to make them feel good just that one day. His clients were also focused on the value of long-term results as the primary component for investment advice. It was the foundation on which he had built his business.

Greg Eason and Bobby Lane valued building relationships with their clients, just as Gary did, but they also knew it took more than the occasional encounter at the cash register to sustain loyalty. If these common clients were exposed to the other's business, they reasoned, it would be good for everyone.

They joined forces by merging their client and customer lists into one database of more than a thousand names and using it to send out invitations to an investment-planning seminar.

Several hundred more flyers about the seminar were placed by the store's cash register. The event has been run multiple times, with both businesses gaining new clients and more frequent business.

When this happens, you automatically attain a greater degree of mind-share, customer loyalty and increased sales. No different from a shop's need to frequently freshen display windows, when customers see "action" in a business, whether it directly involves them or not, the conclusion is: "This must be a dynamic business, one that I am glad to be (or may need to be) connected to, one that I should pay more attention to, or should stop in to see more often. After all, I wouldn't want to miss out on something."

It is no wonder why Gary Bargebuhr has risen to the top ranks in his investment firm. His clients appreciate his efforts to generate goodwill and his focus on trying to give value beyond normal good service and good advice. His efforts take him out of the "me-too" category where most financial advisors reside. Gary is special and his clients know it. He has become "a little bit FAMOUS!"

The Bookstore Alliance

Bill, a financial advisor and devout Christian, saw the local Christian bookstore as the perfect alliance partner. As he explained to the storeowner, they shared the same values, believed in the same theology, supported the same organizations, and more than likely had some of the same clients. Bill wanted to work exclusively with the type of client who shared his values. He made a very convincing argument that an alliance could complement each other's business.

The idea they hit upon was an appreciation event for bookstore customers called "Child's Morning Out" – a thank-you in the form of a free movie for customers' children.

They contacted a movie theater and purchased an entire mid-morning showing of a new biblical-themed, animated children's movie. The event was promoted several weeks in advance with a mailer to the store's customers and also to Bill's clientele. Additional flyers were handed out at the store's checkout counter with every purchase.

The flyers emphasized that the movie was free, but that parents needed to pre-register their children on a certain Saturday from 9 a.m. to noon. As a bonus, the children were encouraged to bring friends with them.

On "registration Saturday" at the store, the response was overwhelming. Phones began ringing and customers began arriving as soon as the doors opened. Within an hour, every seat at the theater had been booked. By noon, two additional showings had been arranged with the theater and all of those seats were taken, too.

More than nine hundred parents registered for the event,

while countless other customers joined in the good vibes created by this gesture of goodwill.

The registration forms – filled out with parents' names, addresses, phone numbers and e-mail addresses – performed two functions. They created a database for future connections and they were used for door-prize drawings the day of the movie.

The cost to the alliance partners was surprisingly affordable. The theater charged just four hundred to five hundred dollars per showing because the facility is normally not open until 1 p.m. Bill hired his church's junior high youth group (contributing two hundred dollars to their summer beach trip fund) to escort the children into the theater as they were dropped off by parents. A local doughnut shop donated free doughnuts (in individual plastic bags with coupons attached). The bookstore gave five- and ten-dollar gift certificates. The theater gave ten movie passes as door prizes, with the winners drawn from a hat onstage after the movie.

The "Child's Morning Out" event is now offered once or twice a year. It has become an identifying business image, a brand mark, uniquely identified with both the bookstore and the financial planner.

The Pumpkin Giveaway
Prospect Name-Acquisition Event

This is an inexpensive activity for acquiring new prospect names and creating market intrigue at the same time.

As Halloween approaches, purchase a cargo-van or truckload of pumpkins. Eight hundred pumpkins will cost you less than three hundred dollars from a wholesaler. You can find the nearest seller through a Yahoo.com search; plug in the words "pumpkin farm," a dash and the name of your city.

Now, choose a school, private school, retirement home, church, or day care center and explain to them your idea for a simple event that features free pumpkins for children and a lot of fun for everyone.

Have that organization coordinate a pumpkin-painting contest during the week, convene a panel of three judges, and announce the five winners. Award each of the winning children a fifty-dollar savings bond, a certificate for free ice cream (provided by a favorite ice cream parlor), movie tickets, book store certificates, etc. Don't be surprised if this goodwill gesture evolves into a newsworthy event, so be sure to have somebody call the newspaper.

Giving away free pumpkins and at the same time capturing the names, addresses and e-mail addresses of parents on a registration card is an easy way to begin a long-term courting strategy. It is a simple way to build a large new roster of targeted prospects – to whom you can now send periodical information about financial subjects such as college savings programs and wealth strategy plans. After all, consistent visibility is what creates credibility. Consider combining your pumpkin giveaway with a Child ID event, especially if holding the event at a school or retirement home that has invited the grandchildren. You will attract more children and increase parent appreciation.

Next year, send an e-mail to announce the annual pumpkin giveaway again, allowing these children to come a day early to get their pumpkins first. That's another good reason to require a registration form with an e-mail address.

Bonus tip: Take digital pictures of the children picking out pumpkins and send an e-photo album to all of the parents. You can download your pictures into a photo album at www.e-relationship.com.

Pumpkin Giveaway Registration Form

Thanks for letting your child participate in the Pumpkin Giveaway. It is an annual event that allows me to express my appreciation to the community and to my clients, most of whom have children.

Please allow me to send information on next year's Pumpkin Giveaway event as well as periodical information on financial subjects such as reducing taxes or investment tips and ideas. Your personal information will not be shared with any other party and you can elect not to receive future information at any time.

Name of Child _____

Parent or Attending Adult (Print)_____

Signature _____

E-mail Address _____

Address _____

Phone _____

The Charity Silent Auction

Many organizations hold silent auctions to raise money for worthy causes. Most of them are held in the evening and target affluent individuals.

The two most common mistakes that most organizations commit are:

- They don't enter their attendees in a permanent database.
- They don't gather attendee e-mail addresses to store for next year's invitations.

Most of these organizations start over every year targeting people to invite. They rarely send a letter or e-mail to attendees announcing the final fundraising results of the evening, thanking them for their participation, and encouraging them to mark their calendars for next year's auction.

Volunteer to register the attendees and do all of the above tasks.

Register the attendees, get their addresses and e-mail addresses, send a letter of thanks on behalf of the organization, announce the results, assemble the database for next year's event (giving a copy to the organization) and offer to send out next year's announcement to assure a good attendance.

Can you drop these names into your personal database? Yes. Many times, no one will care. If they do, remember, you have an entire evening to personally meet these people, shake hands and thank them for attending. The ones you personally interact with and consider great future clients, you certainly have a legitimate right to send a thank-you for attending and include them in your database for further familiarization.

No one is going to object if you handle these names with class and with a focus on giving value first before calling.

The Garden Center Connection

Gardening is the number-one American pastime, and gardeners are the most affluent hobbyists in the country. Garden centers, of course, cherish these middle-upper and upper-income customers, and these are also people that you would like as clients. By helping to brand the garden store deeper into the mind of the customer, you will be a hero.

Nursery and landscaping businesses are very receptive to ideas on how to connect, influence and intensify relationships with their existing client base as well as to connect with new customers. They will welcome your creative ideas. Here is one to start with.

Offer to cosponsor an annual event called "You May Not Live in the Garden of Eden Yet... But We Want to Help You Get There." Put together an evening that features a wine and cheese reception, a spectacular dessert buffet, drawings for gift certificates, and twenty-minute presentations on "enhancing your green thumb" and "increasing the green in your financial portfolio."

Send invitations to the store's client base and also to names in your prospect database. Make it an RSVP event; announce that there is limited seating and that only select friends, customers and clients have been invited. Suggest to the garden shop that you make this a "friends bringing friends" event.

Prospect attraction requires creating high visibility and likeability. Your goal should be to lead your audience to a strong identification of you. To do that requires a local strategy of connection consistency and differentiation. If you're going to achieve high-level success, you must create a belief that you're special and unique relative to the competition.

Relationships don't develop because of what you know about the other person. It requires that the other person also knows something about you. Or as Jerry Acuff and Wally Wood, authors of *The Relationship Edge in Business,* say: "Building a strong business relationship is a process. It's not magic, it's not chemistry, it's not luck, it's a process. Relationships aren't built on mindset or information. Relationships are built on action."

The Annual Convention

You may have an opportunity to participate in an organization's annual convention. But before agreeing to do so, it is imperative that you figure out how to appear unique and receive high-level and distinctive recognition.

It may be even more imperative that you know what not to do. So, let's review that first.

- Do not agree to sponsor the cocktail reception. It is not unique; no one will notice or care; and worst of all, you will have wasted your money. Great marketers don't waste money.

- Do not purchase an advertisement in the convention program. There are far wiser ways to spend your money.

- If your product or service is intangible, non-consumable and can't be demonstrated, do not purchase an exhibition booth in order to pass out brochures. These brochures are discarded as quickly as they are placed into the carry bag – and no, you do not make an impact just because they see your name, or because you think your products or services possess a uniqueness that no one else has. If your product is intangible, a booth is not your answer to marketing.

Now, here are some ideas that are worth your time and money and will make the convention a successful experience for you.

- Work the morning coffee booth. Turn it from a self-serve bar into a full-service coffee bar and have the coffee cups imprinted with your name. (Don't consider just providing coffee cups with a company name imprint. You are the element that needs to be branded. Make sure your name is included in the printing.

- Sponsor a drawing at the coffee booth to be held fifteen minutes before the daily program begins. Provide a stack of small registration forms (name, address and e-mail) and a fishbowl. Give away prizes, like a pound of coffee every month for a year, a dozen doughnuts each month, or a couple copies of Tom Stanley's book, *The Millionaire Next Door*. Name the drawing "The Early Bird Catches the Worm." Note the nametags on the really friendly people who stop by and engage you in conversation. They may be the first people you will want to call on after you add all the names into your prospect database.

- Offer to speak at a breakout session. Title your session to attract attention as a revenue enhancer. Like "Secrets to Reducing Your Employee Benefit Costs while Increasing Employee Satisfaction," or "Secrets the IRS Doesn't Tell You about Reducing Your Taxes," or "Retirement Plans that Employees Love and Yet Give Employers the Biggest Benefit."

- If you didn't get scheduled to conduct an educational breakout session by the organization, offer to pay for an alternative "working lunch" session with a catchy title like those above. Offer to send special invitations to attendees and handle the registration for the breakout lunch. (Report the registration numbers to the association so it won't have to pay for the regularly planned lunches for these people; they will be enticed just by the savings. Make sure this special luncheon is displayed in the program and, if possible, placed on the official registration form. Lunch will cost you about ten dollars per attendee – and it's a great investment even if you have to pay to feed a crowd. Look at the quality perception you created with everyone.

Grabber Letters

There are times when acquiring an appointment with a desired prospect requires an extra push. The most effective way to do this is by creating a memorable experience – the more outrageous the better! It needs to be something that delights, surprises and grabs the attention of the prospect, while producing likeability.

Grabber letters can work miracles, securing appointments with even the most elusive prospect. Here is an example. (Consult your compliance department for appropriate changes before using.) Send the letter in a second-day special delivery envelope and enclose a Floppy Bee Stuffed Animal. (Three to six dollars each; see picture next page.)

Sample "BEE" Grabber Letter

Dear _____,

Wondering what all the BUZZ is about? Or are you so busy that you're overlooking a HONEY of a great opportunity while possibly focusing on the STING of your day-to-day hectic life?

Well, stop a minute. Opportunities come and go, and when you miss them, your future is going to be affected. That's just how life works.

Most people recognize us as the financial specialists here in (town name), with a focus on [pick one of the following]
- *working with small businesses.*
- *creating individualized wealth strategy plans – not just investment advice.*
- *working with entrepreneurs.*

Our objective with our clients is to reduce taxes and maximize after-tax wealth.

That's why most people we contact are agreeable to a short consultation. And here's my guarantee: If you don't come away from that meeting with at least one idea you think has potential for you, I will go away and never return. Yes – I mean never!

Is it worthwhile meeting with me for twenty minutes? Our clients would say so. After all, they're the ones who are creating all the BUZZ. Here's another incentive. You have no idea how many stuffed critters we have – and will send you! – if you don't say "yes" to a short, painless and entertaining twenty-minute meeting. I can assure you it will be enjoyable.

I'll call you in the next few days to schedule a visit. Trust me, it's a wiser choice than figuring out what to do with the zoo of animals that might otherwise come your way!

Sincerely,

Advisor's name

Please… Make ME a little bit FAMOUS

"Make ME a little bit FAMOUS" Notebook

My thoughts on how to apply this chapter's lessons to my business...

_____
_____
_____
_____
_____
_____
_____
_____
_____
_____
_____
_____
_____
_____
_____
_____
_____
_____
_____
_____
_____
_____
_____
_____

"Breaking from the masses doesn't require
differentiation.
It requires exceptional differentiation."

Robert E. Krumroy

Chapter Six

The PACC Model
• Step Three •

Characteristic uniqueness

"Eighty-seven percent of clients that leave [the advisor] do so because of the relationship and not company performance," says Lou Cassara, author of *From Selling to Serving: The Essence of Client Creation.*

While reading this section, pay attention to how the fourth rule of prospect attraction impacts your market perception and client loyalty. What do you do that keeps the relationship alive and fresh on the minds of prospects and clients?

As Lou Cassara says: "Your process of relating to others is your real product."

The Rule of Similar Others*

How it works.
Robert Cialdini,* author of the book *Influence* and a psychologist who studies why people follow the herd, writes that social proof is our strongest influence on taking specific

action. In other words, we are highly influenced by friends, acquaintances and other people we respect. We look at "similar others" when deciding what product to buy or what action to take.

The lesson.
Making sure prospects are aware of your *other* clients may be your strongest influencer when requesting an interview, as well as influencing them to take action during the sales process. With your client's permission, consider creating a listing of clients, especially those who are highly recognizable in your targeted market. Additionally, connecting your clients with other clients, or getting clients to bring friends to events where other clients are present, has a far bigger effect than just the social interaction. It is a validation that you are special, deserving at least to be heard and given serious consideration.

The purpose of implementing Activating Events (Chapter Four, *Step Three*) is to build general personal awareness, increase likeability and accentuate a common linkage to your targeted prospect market. The purpose of Characteristic Uniqueness is to accentuate your differentiated, unique business reputation.

There are, however, carryover benefits in both steps. Many of the ideas you'll see in this chapter will heighten both prospect awareness and client appreciation of you – and will lead them to the conclusion that you are different and outclass the competition. Many of the ideas will also build deep client loyalty (resulting in unexpected new sales, cross-selling opportunities and unsolicited referrals) simply due to the Rule of Reciprocation.

Take this advice seriously. If you don't want to look like all the other "me-too," rather boring financial advisors, do something exceptional. Failure to break from the masses guarantees you will never experience the high level of success that is waiting for those who forge a distinct and unique path.

Following are a number of ideas and stories that will help you create distinction. Find one or several that work for you, adopt or adapt, and watch your market appeal soar to new heights.

The Restaurant Commentary*

Ivan M. Kobey began his career in the stock brokerage industry in the 1970s, transitioning to his current profession as a tax-planning strategist in Scottsdale, Arizona, in 1991. That year, looking for a way to differentiate himself within his field, Ivan hit upon the idea of writing a half-page daily economic update – and putting it in front of diners at local eateries.

He made two hundred copies of his first report and contacted two local restaurants to see if they would place them on tables during the lunch hour.

The rest is history. It wasn't long before he was noted on radio stations and in local news articles as an economic futurist, as well as an economic tax-planning strategist. Ivan's unique initiative created his reputation as being the "expert," a professional who stands out as superior and different.

Today, Ivan gives eight to ten speeches a month, as well as answering weekly calls from around the country. His little commentary is no longer just a local publication. Responding to the many lunchtime readers who didn't want to miss a single edition, he sends the update out by e-mail every day as well as continuing to place it in restaurants.

The Arizona Republic even mentioned his economic update in its review of Scottsdale's prestigious restaurant Molly's-on-Main, as part of the noontime ambience at that restaurant.

His business has flourished. He has answered the question "Why Ivan?" in an occupational field with numerous competitors.

*from Brilliant Strategies and Fatal Blunders by Robert E. Krumroy

KOBEY'S FINANCIAL UPDATE   05\03\00 11:00 AM EST

FINANCIAL NEWS SUMMARY: It's your economy - And - Investors are being confused by the choices - Where to put funds sitting on the side lines - The two year Treasury Note yielding 6.72% - Try to find a CD that is state tax free and yielding almost 6 and 3/4% - 30 year t/bonds yielding 6.04% while the ten year yields 6.32% - That's a 7 week high for the 10 year - Treasuries were hurt by the home sales number published Tuesday - Home sales at the fastest pace in 1 1/2 years - Home sales being driven by expectations the Fed will raise rates, not when, but, by how much - 1/4% or 1/2% - Place your bets - This writer sees another rate increase coming down the path soon after May's increase - Factory orders reported an increase of 2.2% - Analysts polled by Bloomberg News expected an increase - But, only 1.7% - This economy continues to fool many analysts - Does it not make sense that fear of higher prices drives consumers to action - Does to this writer - Does to those who hear me speak - Education is now an export - Foreign students pay to be educated - Buying services - Watch!

NYSE Dow Jones.......- 162.26 pts 10,569	30 yr Fixed Mortgage .... 7 3/4 + 1	
NASDAQ................ - 125.33 pts 3,660	15 yr Fixed Mortgage .... 7 1/2 + 1	
30 Year US Treasury...................... .6.04%	1 year ARM .... 6 3/4 + 1	
Money Market Funds-Banks 3.50%	(Subject to **Market** fluctuation - Origination Fee not included)	
as quoted by: **NORWEST BANK**	quoted by: **Creative Mortgage Solutions, P.C.**	
6 month CD\365 day CD 3.40%	Trends qu-oted by Compak Trading as heard on KFNN Radio Compak Trading 1-800-388-9700	
Tax deferred Annuity 5, 6, 7%	Stocks - Employers in Arizona	

GOLD: .... UP@ $ 278.30	Intel .... - 3	11/16 Motorola................ - 2	American Express .+	11/16
SILVER: .... UP@ $ 5.08	Honeywell .... +	3/16 US West................ -	13/16 Safeway............... -	11/16
PLATINUM: .... DN@ $ 473.00	Banc One............ -	11/16 Home Depot.......... - 2	15/16 Microsoft............. -	15/16

KOBEY CORP A Problem Solving Firm

E-mail: ikobey@kobey.com Web: www.xroadsmall.com/kobey/

480-423-1096   800-280-1096

Sponsored and Paid by: Call: Michael Del Re

Creative Mortgage Solutions, P.C. MB 0902090

Call for info: (602) 728-0324/ Fax (602) 728-0399

1645 East Missouri , Suite 220 Phoenix , AZ. 85016

The Economic Forecast and
Wine-Tasting (or Dessert) Event

Holding an occasional seminar creates no distinct business definition, separating you from the masses. What does work is conducting events that are repeated year after year. Build distinction and a consistent reputation by conducting two events each year, in January and September, for clients and friends.

Who could resist an event called "The Best Investments and Most Extensive Dessert Extravaganza of the Year" or "A Taste of Wine for the Autumn Times – An Investment Update Coupled with Our Almost-Famous Wine-Tasting Event"?

Invite a mutual fund company to send a manager for a portion of the presentation. Having a noted investment professional take part will certainly appease your compliance department. If asked, the mutual fund company will usually pay for the cost of the event, just for the opportunity to get in front of your best clients. And of course encourage your clients to bring their friends.

A wine merchant can be found who will gladly conduct a three- or four-bottle tasting for free. Wine merchants frequently do these events for pharmaceutical representatives, inviting doctors. They will gladly do the same for you.

Don't plan these events randomly. In October, settle on the dates for the following year and print up the schedule on business-card stock to give to clients and prospects. The schedule provides clear proof and validation that your method of supporting your clients is distinctly superior to and different from the competition.

If your compliance department allows it, print the event dates on the back of your business card. Printing the dates and event titles will become your talking point with clients and prospects, another easy way to validate that you are different from the competition.

The "A-List" Birthday Strategy

Every year, make a list of your top twenty to forty clients. The week before a client's birthday, call his or her administrative assistant and ask what day, during the birthday week, your client is free for lunch. Ask the assistant to schedule you into a slot, tell your plan, and swear this person to secrecy.

As time draws near, order a birthday cake personalized with the client's name. On the day of the luncheon, pick it up and make it to their office by 11:30 a.m. Present it by saying it's just something you do for your top clients because you appreciate their business – *and they will just have to get used to it!* Now stand back and enjoy the response. You will definitely go to lunch afterward, but don't be surprised if you're the one being treated.

This will be the first time anyone from the outside has ever taken a birthday cake to your client. The entire office will be spreading the word about you. At lunch with your client, remember to ask, "Do you know someone who isn't a client of mine, but should be? I have some spots left for a few more 'special birthday' clients and would love your help in identifying candidates."

This idea can generate lots of recognition beyond the office as well as tremendously profitable lists of referrals.

In one case, the secretary of the birthday client called the newspaper in their small town to be on hand when the advisor arrived. The paper subsequently ran a photo of the client and advisor with this caption: "Some Financial Advisors Do More Than Just Give Financial Advice!"

The publicity was great; even better was that the advisor's

structured strategy plan put him well on the way to becoming the differentiated "identity brand" in his local market.

The Business Card Luggage Tag

Mark is an advisor who is always looking for a marketing edge. He rarely misses seeing how an idea may apply to his business.

One week, Mark was staying at a Marriott Courtyard in the Boston area. Though a quality hotel, this particular Marriott Courtyard is always striving to find ways to surprise and delight customers. They know it isn't enough to be seen as just another "me-too" hotel, claiming to provide nicer accommodations.

Marriott Courtyard has numerous strategies for creating distinction. One "little extra" this hotel added was to request business cards when guests checked in. When Mark was checking out, the desk clerk handed him a luggage tag. In actuality, it was his business card, but now laminated and attached to a luggage strap. On the back of the laminated card were the hotel's name, phone number, and a thank-you message.

Brilliant idea... and cheap! A lamination machine at Office Depot runs about forty-nine dollars and each tag costs about ten cents to produce. Assembly time is less than a minute.

Mark decided to adopt this procedure. He now asks prospects and clients for business cards. When he sends a thank-you note for their business (or just for meeting with him), he includes a freshly produced luggage tag. Clients like this idea so much, they often ask for extra tags, and Mark is always willing to oblige.

It doesn't take that much to create distinction in your marketplace. You just need to give it some thought and follow through.

Interactive Association Client Briefings

If you want to build visible dominance within an occupational association, these are the components you should incorporate to build and maintain market preference:

- Attend every association meeting and event. This keeps you visible and also informed about your market segment.

- Connect with the entire membership at least eight times a year with a business communication such as E-Relationship's E-Financial Storyboards (www.e-relationship.com).

- Write a quarterly or biannual article for the association magazine or newsletter. (Many financial companies have ghostwritten articles available.)

- Send out a client/prospect evaluation e-Checklist annually. The questions should allow recipients to request information on financial topics (resulting consequently in numerous raise-your-hand requests as well as accentuating your business reputation).

- Conduct an interactive client briefing at least twice a year with different representative businesses or clients for the purpose of just listening and learning. An interactive client/prospect briefing is when you invite a market segment prospect to talk about what is going on in their market and answer some prepared market questions. Your job is to ask questions, manage the discussion and bring out everyone's viewpoints. The dialogue should yield insights into their needs and lift your reputation above the competition.

A typical letter requesting an interactive briefing would go something like this:

Dear _____,

As you may be aware, your (name of industry) is a market segment that our firm specializes in. For us to keep current with your industry, every year we schedule two dinner meetings to casually visit with two different, strategically representative companies. Our objective is to continue learning in our specialty area so that we can continue to respond appropriately to client needs.

(Optional sentence)
The executive director of your XYZ association, Mr./Ms. _____, recommended we contact you and suggested that your input would complement our research needs.

As a representative company, we are inviting you to join us for a very special dinner at (location). The only thing we will ask of you is to discuss what is changing in your industry. Our objective is to keep current with the world you conduct business in, the competitive environment, and the daily challenges you face. We will probably have a few questions to ask you that will help us gain a better understanding of your industry and special needs. Extensive preparation is not necessary.

We would also like to extend invitations to your attorney, your CPA, one of your key people, and one of your primary suppliers. We will make sure you incur no professional fees from your advisors. This may be a way for you to say thank-you as your special guests to a very nice event, and an additional way for us to get perspectives about your industry. I am sure you will find their insights as interesting as we do.

(Optional sentence)
Your spouse is also more than welcome and is sure to find the evening delightful.

Three persons from our office plan to attend. This is our most effective way to maintain a cutting-edge specialization within your industry that benefits everyone. We certainly hope you will accept.

I will call in the next few days to verify a date and to get the names of guests we can invite on your behalf. Thank you!

What is the result of conducting these briefings? First, your competition doesn't do them. Therefore, you create an immediate impression that you are different, unique and in fact "specializing" in a narrow market. Second, the association director will become your advocate and talk about your specialized focus during board meetings with fellow members, etc. Plus – remember that big potential prospect you wanted to meet with but didn't know how to get the appointment? Well, here's your chance to ask the association director to call in advance and essentially secure a "yes" to your dinner invitation.

Interactive client briefings work. They accentuate your business distinction. They provide the best opportunity to meet with the best prospects. They produce your best advocate within the organization (i.e., the executive director). They open doors. They create high-level visibility to all members. They establish your uniqueness. They create a visible competitive advantage.

Annual Association e-Checklist

Delivering your uniqueness to your fellow association members is imperative if you want to become highly recognized and dominant. Even if your fellow association members know you are in the financial service's field, most of them don't know what you do. An annual or quarterly checklist can help accentuate your professional stature and identify areas in which they may express an interest. Here is an example of an annual e-checklist message (www.e-relationship.com) that links them to a five or ten question e-checklist.

Dear _____,

You and I both belong to the (insert name: e.g., Chamber of Commerce, homebuilder association). Many members consider us to be unique and distinct with our financial specialty focused on (e.g., the construction industry). They also tell us they like to receive our periodic financial updates–often providing ideas for saving taxes and increasing wealth. Therefore, here is the questionnaire I send out twice a year. It takes just a minute to fill it out and will tell me exactly what kind of financial information you are interested in and would be most valuable to you. Thank you so much for your interest.

To access the checklist, click this secure, virus-protected link. (It is not a download or attachment.)

I look forward to seeing you at upcoming meetings and appreciate getting your feedback.

Wondering why frequent connection works - with some people responding instantly and others maybe six to twelve months later? Consider the hotdog vendor. He sets up his cart, always on the same block. The first day, he makes some sales; that's a given. A month later, other people are buying who had been standing back and just observing. They even trust him, because he connects with his audience frequently, often every day.

The lesson? The hotdog vendor's "prospects," having been greeted numerous times, wished Happy St. Patrick's Day and Happy Thanksgiving, and maybe engaged in conversation while waiting for the traffic light to change, decide they "know" this fellow and like him. They even trust him, because he connects with his audience every day.

Think about how many people you casually know who really don't know what you do. Parents of children on your child's soccer team. People you repeatedly see in your daily encounters. Members of your church or synagogue. Referrals for which you never secured an appointment.

What have you done with all those names? Creating a series of connections that builds your likeability and your business image eventually creates a compelling attraction, much like the hotdog vendor.

The Top 50 Theater Event

Purchase an entire performance at a local theater (play) production. Invite your top fifty clients and their guests. You can purchase group tickets and hold a reception before the event. A wine merchant may be more than happy to provide a wine tasting. Purchasing a few trays of finger foods would be inexpensive and appreciated.

The Social/Party Event

Choose to do an event, make it memorable and make it annually predictable. Consistency counts when building a reputation for being distinctly different from the competition.

Ideas that work are as simple as...

- a NCAA basketball championship party
- a Super Bowl party with beer and giant sub sandwiches
- a Kentucky Derby mint julep party

You could also get creative and make your own event, such as "Croquet and Chardonnay – An Evening of Fun and Merriment." The more distinctive the event, the more special the client feels. Even those who can't attend will feel connected.

Remember: People want to be connected to – and will build deep loyalties to – people whose uniqueness is most pronounced.

The Huge-Impact Magazine Idea

Here's a clever and inexpensive idea for making a lasting impression with clients you have just sold, as well as your top ten, twenty or forty clients and others who are continual sources for referrals.

Purchase a magazine subscription for each of these individuals and follow these instructions for filling out the order form.

Put the recipient's address where indicated, but don't fill in their name. Instead, on the "first name" line, put "From." On the "last name" line, put your own first initial, followed by a period and your last name.

In other words, if your name is Sam Jones, the mailing label on the magazine received by your client will read: "From S. Jones." This means that at least twelve times a year, your client will see that label and be reminded of you. (This won't get you in trouble with the post office. The mail carrier doesn't care whose name is on the label.)

The magazines you choose can be consumer oriented in nature, such as *Consumer Reports,* or directed to travel, such as Condé Nast Traveler, or directed to personal interests, such as *Field & Stream* for the outdoorsman or *American Baby* for new parents. Many subscriptions cost less than twelve dollars a year, and the appreciation, continual visibility and deep loyalty this simple little idea builds will result in numerous additional sales and referrals.

Test this idea with ten of your best clients. I think you'll love the results. Making a huge impact just doesn't get any easier than this.

Distinction Identifiers

A distinction identifier describes what you want your prospects to think. It is the initial qualifier that distinguishes you from your competitors.

How essential is this? As author Harry Beckwith says in *Selling the Invisible:* "If no prospect can describe your position, you do not have one."

Identifying the core message of your distinctiveness with a brief sentence or phrase can become a central theme of your uniqueness to your market segment. It is something you can put on your business card and as a tagline after your name when sending letters and e-mail.

An identifier can be simple or clever, but it definitely needs to separate you from the pack. Done right, it can go a long way toward creating a perception of higher service, expertise and specialty – yours!

Decide what your specialty focus is going to be and then make a distinctive statement that offers a unique appeal to your market. Such as:

- "Seniors ONLY, My Specialty"
- "Business Owners ONLY, My Exclusive Focus"
- "Significant Investments ONLY"
- "Reducing Taxes. Increasing After-Tax Wealth"
- "When Reducing Taxes Matters"
- "Korean Only Financial, When an Exclusive Focus Makes a Difference"

Be specific. Stay away from weak cliché statements like "Plan Now. Secure Your Future" or "Helping You Plan for Your

Future." They imply nothing special about you.

Just make sure that you can deliver what you promise. Statements that are true about what you do, says Harry Beckwith in *Selling the Invisible,* "will make your word-of-mouth more effective."

Senior Market Financial Consultant

John began his career in the insurance and investment field eight years ago. His first year was very good, but he wanted a higher level of success and he wanted it to come faster than it had for other agents in his company.

The next year, John took the plunge and redirected his business activity solely to the senior market. It was such a success that he began his third year vowing never again to work with any clients under the age of fifty-five. He made no exceptions, even turning away a client's brother who was just a few months shy of being fifty-five!

John was just that determined to maintain his focus. And it turned out to be absolutely the right decision.

Today, John conducts two seminars a month. One is on "Preventing Identity Theft for Senior Citizens," which is usually co-sponsored by a sales-neutral organization such as a hospital, senior center or church organization. The other is titled "How Seniors Financially Screw up Their Retirement and How to Unscrew It."

The events are held the first Tuesday and Thursday of the month, 10 a.m. to noon. The venue for the first one is the co-sponsoring organization's facility. The other is held at a fine restaurant (never a hotel!), and includes a very nice lunch after the seminar. He seats six people to a table and offers door prizes. The events are so much fun, many attendees ask permission to bring friends to the next one. (This "Friends Bringing Friends" motif has increased attendance by five or six people every month.)

Before starting his entry into this market, John assembled

about six thousand names of prospects fitting the profile of his ideal client: a homeowner fifty-five to seventy-five years old with an annual income of more than fifty thousand dollars. That task took two months of focused work. Now, every month he sends out invitations to these six thousand people, replenishing the database with referrals as prospects become clients.

Two years ago, John also began collecting e-mail addresses. Though he sends out invitations by regular mail and e-mail – he was amazed to find that more than fifty percent of the senior citizens prefer e-mail. He also sends them a monthly financial e-newsletter.

On top of that, John runs two "teaser advertisements" once or twice a month in the local weekly newspaper. The ads cost about one hundred fifty dollars per run. The teaser is not about the seminars, but simply exclaims a message that most senior citizens are paying more in taxes than they should because of critical mistakes in their finances. There's a toll-free number to call for a free booklet. This simple little ad brings in ten to fifteen requests per month.

John also e-mails the teaser to his prospect list, resulting in thirty to fifty requests a month for information. Follow-up phone calls bring twenty attendees to his seminars, along with numerous appointments.

You might be shocked at how audacious John is when it comes to appointments. First of all, he sets them up for 10:15, 11:45, 1:15, 2:45, and occasionally 4:15. It might sound odd to you, but John believes this encourages people to arrive on time. Clients who are more than ten minutes late absolutely won't get in to see him that day. They're politely asked by John's assistant to reschedule and to be on time for the next appointment.

John is a stickler about respect for his time because he extends an extraordinarily high level of respect to his clients. He reserves premier parking spaces right at the front entrance for them (with their name prominently displayed). In the lobby they find a welcome sign with their name. In the office, the receptionist greets them by name, as does everyone they come into contact with.

If you do business with John, you receive flowers after the sale. Regardless of any interview's outcome, he sends a handwritten note to each person immediately after a meeting and personally walks clients to their cars and thanks them.

It goes on and on. He calls all clients on their birthdays. He never delegates this task, not even when he's out of town. When asked how in the world he has time for this, he responds: "I don't have time *not* to call them." He believes that the smallest differences are all about his reputation, about who he is, and about his uniqueness as a differentiated service provider.

At the end of his third year, John quadrupled his income. In the most recent year, his commissions topped six hundred thousand dollars.

Four universal lessons can be derived from John's strategy:

- No business can generate a high level of success in today's market if it is not differentiated from the competition.

- Non-transactional seminars build trust, making it easy to subsequently invite the same people to a transactional event (which they originally might have been hesitant to attend).

- You can't implement a highly effective familiarization strategy unless you know the names of the specific prospects you want to attract and set a strategy to maintain consistent ongoing contact.

- A highly successful practice requires systematization to establish visible definition and differentiation.

Think about what types of experiences capture your attention. People never focus their attention on something that is similar to what they're accustomed. They notice what looks unique and different. Playing a "me-too" game is a mediocre proposition in the financial industry. Build a differentiated distinction. Make it extraordinarily delightful and then communicate it to the same audience over and over. You cannot over-communicate your difference. It's what makes you a little bit famous.

"Make ME a little bit FAMOUS" Notebook

My thoughts on how to apply this chapter's lessons to my business…

_____

_____

_____

_____

_____

_____

_____

_____

_____

_____

_____

_____

_____

_____

_____

_____

_____

_____

_____

_____

_____

_____

_____

_____

_____

_____

_____

"Frequent connection is the foundation
for becoming a little bit famous."

Robert E. Krumroy

The PACC Model
• Step Four •

CONSISTENT CONTACT

Visibility is the hallmark of branding. It's the king of all four steps for creating market dominance, and it's your greatest leverage point.

Don't make the mistake of having a great product, great knowledge and great selling skills, but not having a defined strategy for building high-level consistent connection with your local market prospect and client.

Let's take a look at why consistent connection is so important.

The Rule of Consistent Contact

How it works.
We increase other people's assumption of our personal expertise and uniqueness with repeated contact. Society bestows the label of greatest expert on the person – *not the company* – who is locally noticed the most in any category of service business.

The lesson.

Accentuating your business image and building presence and prestige require that you be seen frequently. E-mail is your friend; use it a lot. Half of the e-mail you send to prospects and clients should be non-transactional: holiday greetings, photo albums, etc. Even if e-mail messages aren't always opened, having people see your name frequently pop up on their computer screens will position you above the competition.

Creating a consistent contact strategy that delivers you to your prospect audience should be your top priority in sales. Most financial professionals have a client database, but you also need to build a significant prospect database and use it. There simply is no other method in today's market to attain high-level success.

Current sales psychology says it takes twelve to eighteen contacts per year to build meaningful "shelf life" in people's minds. That may sound like a lot, but it is a fact. You can never gain a sustained advantage in your market without being more visible than the competition. Now, let's explore methods that will work for you and, just as important, those you need to avoid.

Are Traditional Newsletters Beneficial?

You expect financial companies to send out annual reports and the occasional newsletter or magazine – but don't confuse these items with creating prospect attraction or providing a competitive advantage. Their impact validates to clients that your company is still around, but if sent to prospects, the impact might actually be unfavorable. To a prospect, they appear very commercial and impersonal, even if your picture is on the front of them.

I'm pretty certain that most newsletters sent to prospects (not clients) are immediately tossed in the trash. Isn't that your typical response to unsolicited newsletters you receive in the mail? Even if you disagree, most newsletters offer very little personal "likeability" value. They don't profile you personally or accentuate your personal distinction within the market. They don't do the job you need them to do, which is drawing prospects to conclude that they know you, like you and trust you.

Is Print or TV Advertising
an Effective Strategy?

Financial companies spend millions of dollars on media advertising, even though the general population can't tell one ad from another. It sure is a lot of money to spend on something that your hoped-for audience finds overwhelmingly easy to tune out entirely.

There are two simple reasons why companies continue to use ads. The first one is that advertisements help increase stock price, due to their ability to increase institutional buying. The second one is that advertising is a defensive response. One big company knows that another big company is spending one percent of profits on national advertising and feels compelled to respond in like fashion for fear of falling behind (even though there is no proof of that effect).

Yes, the budget process for advertising is that simple. It is all subjective and defensive. Not one company can quantify the effect a national advertising budget has on sales. National advertising does have its benefits, such as enhancing corporate image and name recognition, but it is not a factor in creating new prospect attraction for you.

And, sorry, but it's just the same with local ads. They may be beautiful and clever and colorful – but they don't work. They do not grab hold of local prospects by making you look distinct and likeable in a meaningful way. They are not creating a compelling attraction – *and they are not making you money.*

The only exception that might be worthwhile is to place an ad in the publication of an association you belong to – but only if you already have a high profile. Before doing that, however, consider spending your money on an activating event. Your association's golf tournament will provide a much higher payback, especially if you follow up by sending a photo album of the event to prospects you meet there.

What about Web Sites?

There are reasons why you might want your own Web site, but don't create one believing it will open doors to new prospects or give you a marketing advantage over the competition. Nobody is surfing the Internet's three billion Web sites hoping to discover a great financial professional.

Prospects whom you have not personally met are not going to spend time reviewing your Web site, even if you sent them the link or included it at the bottom of an e-mail message. And neither will most prospects take the time to download a video presentation causing them to sit silently while conveying a financial crisis message.

Web sites are useful as places your clients (not prospects) can visit for self-service: to check investment account balances, request forms for medical claims, etc. Other than that, they are validation components, providing confidence that you are legitimate. But they do not create prospect attraction.

What About Cold Prospect Pre-Approach Letters?

Remember when getting mail was a pleasurable experience? No more! Being bombarded with two to three thousand pieces of junk mail each year has certainly ended that. Most of it goes in the trashcan unopened.

This general disaffection for mass mailings means that a pre-approach letter sent through the U.S. Mail to a cold prospect is almost guaranteed to make a poor first impression. It won't help build personal affection or presence. It may even be harmful, with prospect-recipients now having enough information to decide not to take your phone call, having already decided not to meet with you.

Using the mail is expensive and time-consuming; it's almost impossible to do consistent mailings and build positive awareness of you. If you are going to send a letter, make sure it is a strong referral letter or a humorous grabber letter with a significant insert. *(See Chapter Six.)*

What about E-mail?

We've all had the experience of a prospect saying "no" to an appointment. A typical response, unfortunately, is to place their name in a callback file and try again in six or twelve months... expecting that something magical has happened in the meantime and the prospect is now ready and willing.

This kind of wishful thinking is insane. Whatever happened to the courting process, favorably influencing the prospect before calling back? The sixth rule for prospect attraction demonstrates a much better method for courting, and then reconnecting, after someone turns you down.

The Rule of Big to Small

How it works.
When turned down for an appointment (the big request), you can almost always get the person to agree to a smaller request.

The lesson.
Never lose a prospect. With every contact, your job is to move the prospect one step closer to a face-to-face sales encounter.

Here's an example of a Big-to-Small Retreat:

> *"I fully understand. I certainly don't want to push you. However, even though an appointment isn't appropriate at this time, would it be okay if I include you in some of the periodic information briefs I e-mail to my clients? If you see anything you want more details on, there is always a request button. So, would that be okay? Great! Just give me your e-mail address."*

After getting the e-mail address, here is an optional close:

> *"Thanks for your e-mail address. I certainly will respect your time and what I send to you. After you have had a chance to learn more about what I do, I'm hoping you'll be interested in having lunch with me. So would it be okay if I called you back in a few months?"*

E-mail is the only affordable and effective way to create a non-present consistent contact strategy. It's the preferred way for more than eighty percent of business owners to communicate, and those high percentages are reflected across the general population and amid some of the most desirable demographics (such as high-income households, seniors, and families with young children). The Gartner research organization recently estimated that e-mail is two hundred and eighty-four percent more effective in getting a message across than traditional direct mailings.

Sure, a lot of e-mails get tossed just like regular mail. But if the client or prospect knows your name and recognizes you as the sender or recognizes the commonality of a group displayed on the subject line (such as "Fellow Dallas Chamber Member – Important Info"), your e-mail will be opened and read.

That's why your job is to go public, get involved, get recognized within your identified prospect audience, and become a little bit famous. E-mail is not a marketing system in itself – just a connection tool in your process of creating prospect attraction.

If you're going to use e-mail, be sure not to use your

company's name (corporate or local) for the sender ID. Prospects automatically have an aversion to that, thinking they're getting financial propaganda. Even e-mailed birthday cards with a company "signature" in the "From" line or on the e-card will get this treatment. Always use a personal name.

Besides sending e-cards throughout the year, you should use e-mail to refresh clients and prospects about what you do. Even if they've heard it before, sending a new message on the same topic (but in a different format) makes a huge impact. They may not have been ready for your offering last year, but now maybe they are.

E-Relationship™ is an electronic tool many professionals use to stay in touch with clients. It's the number-one compliance-approved e-connection tool in the financial industry. It can be programmed to automatically send e-birthday, e-anniversary and e-holiday cards to people in your database. There are also yearly financial e-Annual Review Checklists, quarterly e-Mini Checklists and e-Financial Storyboards available to e-mail to clients and prospects at any time. The e-Financial Storyboards all allow the recipient to ask for more information on any of the fifty topics you choose to send, notifying you when a request for more information is made. It's a great way to identify sales that would normally go undetected.

Example of E-Financial Storyboard

UMBRELLA POLICY

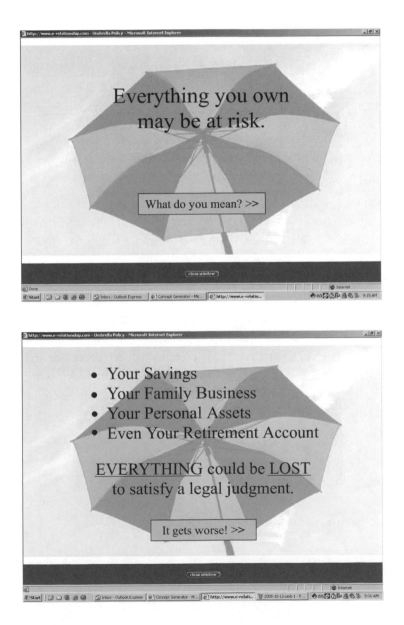

Example of E-Financial Storyboard

UMBRELLA POLICY (continued)

When an injury involves you or a family member and another person

(a traffic accident, a passenger in your car, pool accident, children at your house, slander, etc.)

Your **attorney defense fees alone** can be six figures… devastating your savings…**regardless** of whether you **WIN** or **LOSE**!

It gets worse! >>

close window

An inexpensive umbrella policy can provide the added protection, providing money for legal expenses and legal judgments!

EXPENSIVE?
We think that it's inexpensive…
Not having it…THAT'S EXPENSIVE!

Please provide additional information>>   Exit >>

close window

Example of E-Financial Storyboard

FINANCIAL STRATEGIES

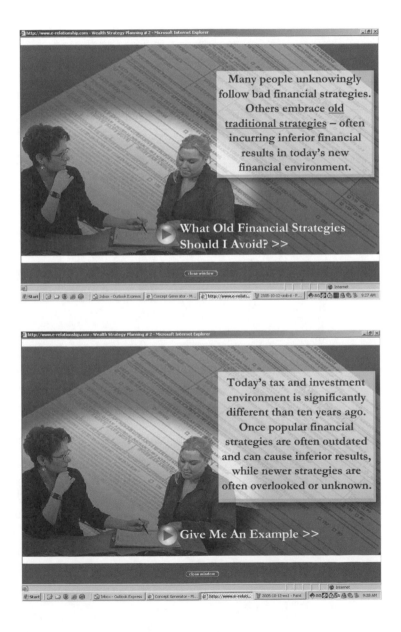

Example of E-Financial Storyboard

FINANCIAL STRATEGIES (continued)

Example of E-Financial Storyboard

ASSET MANAGEMENT

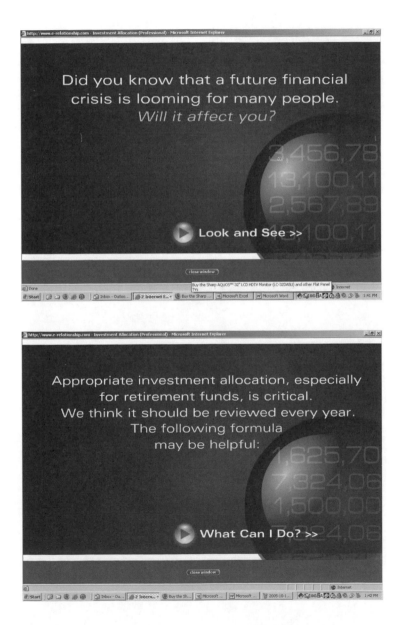

Example of E-Financial Storyboard

ASSET MANAGEMENT (continued)

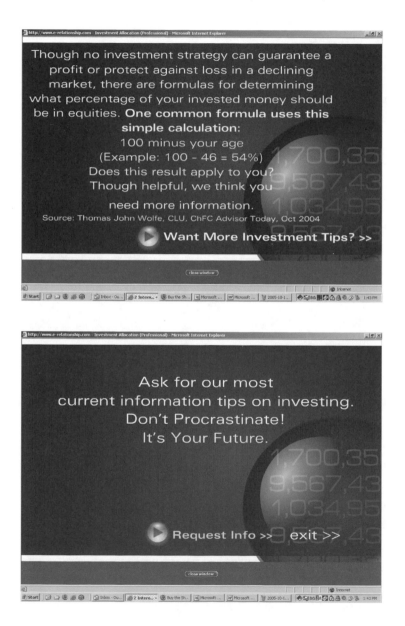

Example of E-Financial Storyboard

RETIREMENT

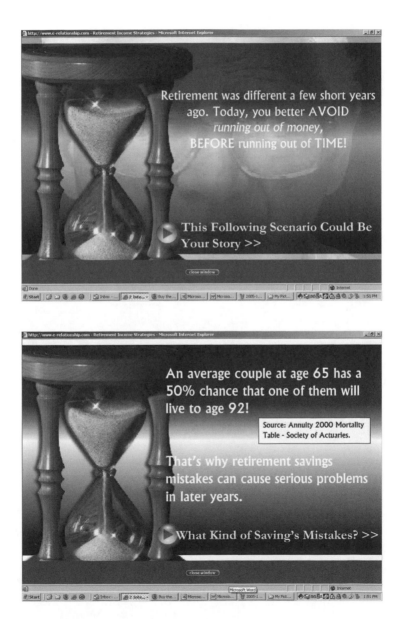

Example of E-Financial Storyboard

RETIREMENT (continued)

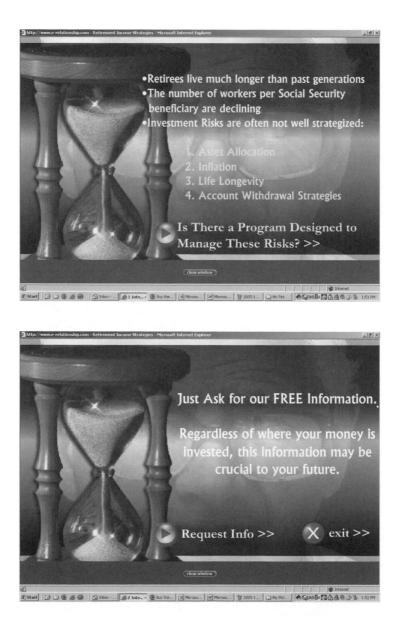

A Prospect-Attraction Success Story

Mark is an E-Relationship™ subscriber. He uses it to send an annual review e-Checklist, four E-Financial Storyboards and all manner of greeting e-cards to his two hundred thirty clients and eleven hundred prospects. About six percent respond by asking for more information throughout the year, with many turning into new sales.

Not only does Mark touch his database audience twelve to fourteen times a year, he also shows up at area hospitals once a month to conduct an evening clinic on the topic of "Medicare, Health and Money – the Facts and the Secrets." That's where he got the names of people ages fifty-five and up for his prospect database. The marketing departments in the participating hospitals do all of the promotion and advertising for the clinics. Along with offering yoga, exercise, painting and health classes, it's part of what they do to make their hospitals community-friendly.

But this advisor's high-profile strategy doesn't stop there. He's a member of the Assisted-Living Association, which represents more than one hundred eighty homes for the elderly in his part of the state. At the golf tournament that precedes the association's annual conference, he's the guy at the ninth hole handing out beer, soft drinks and bottled water to golfers. He also takes digital pictures of the foursomes and conducts a hilarious driving contest involving marshmallows. The winner of each foursome takes home a new car (actually a matchbox Jaguar he hides in his pocket!). Mark gathers all of the golfers' e-mail addresses and gets permission to e-mail them the event photo album he puts together, plus information on his seminar and occasional financial briefs.

Mark's involvement in the community goes even further. He

is a volunteer instructor for a monthly two-hour introductory course for seniors on "How to Use E-mail." The seminar is held at a community college and attracts fifty people each time.

What do you think? Will these new e-mail users open Mark's e-invitation to his quarterly seminar… access his greeting e-cards… and read his financial e-briefings on long-term care and how to avoid unnecessary taxes?

And wait – there's even more. Mark's newest project involves co-presenting a series of seminars with an eldercare attorney on "Preventing Identity Theft – The New Senior Crisis in America." Now, that's marketing!

This savvy advisor is creating a whole lot of goodwill and transitioning that goodwill into annuities, insurance and investment sales. People grant appointments to those they like, and likeability precedes preference. Getting meaningful-ly connected is your top strategy for exceptional growth.

Pushing financial information out to prospects is a far superior way to build local market awareness than trying to get them to go to your Web site. Technology is always evolving. No longer in opposition to relationship building, it is a relationship enhancer. E-Relationship™ will differentiate you from the competition. Visit www.e-Relationship.com to learn more about this dynamic tool.

"Make ME a little bit FAMOUS" Notebook

My thoughts on how to apply this chapter's lessons to my business…

_____

_____

_____

_____

_____

_____

_____

_____

_____

_____

_____

_____

_____

_____

_____

_____

_____

_____

_____

_____

_____

_____

_____

_____

_____

_____

_____

_____

"Most advisors want to change their outcome,
but are unwilling to change their process.
Don't let that happen to you."

Robert E. Krumroy

Chapter Eight

Putting It All Together

Prospect Attraction is no longer about your company's name recognition, your product or your sales training. It is about the strategy that connects and keeps connecting you to prospective clients in a way that makes you approachable, likeable, trusted and distinct from the competition.

Following the Prospect Attraction Model will allow you to climb the Business Relationship Ladder™ and reach your maximum potential. This diagram (on page 168) illustrates why each of the eight steps discussed in this book is critical.

Steps 1-3 are simple connecting steps; steps 4-8 are bonding steps – the steps that make prospect access significantly easier and more welcoming. Sadly, many advisors are still contacting the majority of their prospects on the bottom three rungs, giving most prospects no compelling reason to say yes to an appointment. It doesn't have to be like this.

The Business Relationship Ladder™ doesn't always get scaled in the precise order shown, and ascending it may take many months. But for your best clients, all of the rungs will eventually get stepped on.

Please… Make ME a little bit FAMOUS

The Business Relationship Ladder™

PROSPECT CONCLUSION:
Friendship and Business Should Be Combined

My Consistent Contact Builds Confidence

Sees My Business
Characteristic / Uniqueness

Has A Unique Experiential Encounter
(Activating Event)

Discovers We Have a
Social Connection or Belief Commonality

Knows My Business Affiliation

Knows My Name

Doesn't Know Me

CONTACT FREQUENCY

© 2005 Identity Branding, Inc, All rights reserved
Identity Branding, Inc. 2007 Yanceyville Street, Box 2, Greensboro, NC 27405 I.800.851.8169
www.e-relationship.com   www.identitybranding.com

Sales, appointments and personal fulfillment will all increase if you take the time to build a prospect-attraction strategy, allowing your prospects to ascend the Relationship Ladder by encompassing these four steps:

1. Build a **significant prospect database** of people you would like to do business with, not just today but over the next five years.

2. Create a strategy to deliver highly visible **activating events** throughout the year, endearing these prospects to you.

3. Decide on components you will adopt to make your business reputation **characteristically unique,** relative to the competition.

4. Make **consistent contact** twelve to eighteen times a year.

On a personal note, studying prospect attraction in the financial field over the last five years has been a challenging journey. No one else in the financial industry has gathered as many facts, tested as many theories and observed as many advisors in different companies.

Company training directors and local marketing directors are often referred to as the people in charge of marketing. But their jobs are so multi-focused, it's no wonder they only have a surface knowledge, or that they confuse Web sites, agency promotional events, brochures, newsletters and a multitude of other imposters as local prospect-attraction marketing. None of these provide significant impact for individual agents and advisors trying to position themselves in the local market. And even though it's easy to engage these people in a discussion about the concept of differentiation, few if any have real examples for advisors to copy or adopt.

In summary, then, having the rare opportunity to focus on this one single item – Prospect Attraction – has been a privilege. It is far more misunderstood than I ever imagined! The lessons have been many, but it has been thrilling and rewarding to help advisors build strategies and watch their production soar.

One final caution. In my studies, I have found that most advisors want to change their outcome, but are unwilling to change their process. Success doesn't happen by chance; it happens because of bravery – the willingness to build and stick to an action plan that is different from the norm and outclasses the competition.

With that being said, I leave you with six words that, if implemented, will change your world and your sales results.

Just build it. They will come.

"Make ME a little bit FAMOUS" Notebook

My thoughts on how to apply this chapter's lessons to my business…

_____

_____

_____

_____

_____

_____

_____

_____

_____

_____

_____

_____

_____

_____

_____

_____

_____

_____

_____

_____

_____

_____

_____

_____

_____

_____

_____

Please… Make ME a little bit FAMOUS

Building an Identity Branding
Business Model

1. Create a **Prospect Database** of individual prospects (minimum five hundred names).

   - Decide how you will get actual names.
   - How many names will you accumulate each month, quarter, year?
   - End-of-year goal?
   - What database will you accumulate these names in?

2. What **Activating Events** will you use to heighten your local awareness?

3. What **Characteristic Uniqueness** will you adopt to build a differentiated business reputation?

4. What means of **Consistent Contact** will you employ?

5. Set review dates to determine progress.

   First review date: _____

   Second review date: _____

   Third review date: _____

   Fourth review date: _____

Please… Make ME a little bit FAMOUS

About the Author

Robert E. Krumroy, known as "the Branding Coach," is president and CEO of Identity Branding, Inc. He is also founder and creator of the e-mail marketing tools www.e-relationship.com, www.agent-recruiting.com and www.my-ecustomer.com. Identity Branding is dedicated to helping financial sales professionals create a visibly distinct and unique local market presence, a perception of superior value – eventually creating an almost unfair competitive advantage for themselves. Once accomplished, these professionals can thrive, successfully attracting prospects and outclassing the competition.

With twenty-five years of experience in the financial services industry, the author qualified sixteen times as a National Management Award winner and built his financial service firm into one of the one hundred largest in the country. *Please… Make ME a Little Bit FAMOUS* is his fourth book. Previous titles by the author include *Identity Branding – Distinct or Extinct*, *Identity Branding – Revisited and Brilliant Strategies and Fatal Blunders*. He also has authored hundreds of columns and magazine articles.

He has served on national teaching faculties and is a highly sought-after speaker, giving more than one hundred clinics and speeches each year to some of the largest companies both in the United States and internationally. He has been introduced often as one of the best marketing minds in the country.

For more information:

www.identitybranding.com

www.e-relationship.com

www.agent-recruiting.com

You can also call, e-mail, write or fax:

Identity Branding Inc.
2007 Yanceyville Street, Box 2
Greensboro, NC 27405

Toll free: 1.800.851.8169
Fax: 1.336.303.7318
E-mail: Bob@identitybranding.com

References &
Acknowledgments

Acuff, Jerry and Wood, Wally. *The Relationship Edge in Business.* Hoboken, NJ: John Wiley & Sons: 2004.

Beckwith, Harry. *Selling the Invisible.* New York: Warner Books, 1997.

Cassara, Lou. *From Selling to Serving: The Essence of Client Creation.* Chicago: Dearborn, 2004.

Cialdini, Robert. *Influence – Science and Practice.* Needham Heights, MA: Allyn & Bacon, 2001.

> Note: There was significant influence on formulating our rules for prospect attraction from the research in this book. It is an extensive study of how behavior is influenced. I highly recommend this book.

Godin, Seth. *All Marketers are Liars.* New York: Penguin Group, 2005.

Krumroy, Robert E. *Brilliant Strategies and Fatal Blunders.* Greensboro, N.C.: I-B Publishing, 2002.

Littell, Robert S. *The Heart and Art of NetWeaving.* Atlanta, GA: NetWeaving International Press, 2003.

Misner Ph.D., Ivan R. and Morris, Jeff. *Givers Gain – The BNI Story.* St. Paul, MN: Paradigm Publishing: 2004.

Prince, Russ and File, Karen. *Marketing Through Advisors.* Cincinnati, OH: National Underwriter, 1996.

Index

(Key Words and Phrases)

To Order Books

Please mail or fax this form to the address below, or use the electronic order form found at www.identitybranding.com.

_____ copies at $24.95 each = _____
($24.95 US; $32.95 CAN)

Plus $4.00 shipping/handling = _____
($4.00 US; $6.00 CAN)

Total Enclosed = _____

Please send book(s) to:

Name_____

Address _____

City _____ State _____ Zip _____

Method of payment:
❏ VISA   ❏ MasterCard   ❏ AMEX

Credit Card number:_____

Expiration Date _____

Phone Number (   ) _____

Card Holder's Signature _____

Order on our Web site or by sending credit card, check or money order to:

Identity Branding
2007 Yanceyville Street, Box 2
Greensboro, NC 27405

Fax: 336-303-7318
E-mail: info@identitybranding.com
www.identitybranding.com

*If you're interested in growing your practice
to a new level, this is for you!*

High Performance
Marketing Coaching Program
(Limited to 30 attendees Each Session)

Four Sessions per Year

**A 6-Month INTENSIVE
Coaching Program**
- One Initial Full Day
  Personal Design and
  Planning Session
- One Full Day Practice
  Management Session
  (4th Month)
- Six Follow-up Coaching
  Phone Sessions
- On-Call 24/7 Support
  and Coaching for Six
  Months

Who should enroll in
this program?
- Only those advisors who
  are seriously committed
  to moving to the next
  level of success – those
  who want a serious
  production increase and
  are willing to build
  plans, be coachable and
  accept feedback on
  performance.

For Details:
1-800-851-8169

THIS
WILL CHANGE
YOUR LIFE!

You will learn to reorganize and refocus on:

- Managing the five critical performance areas
- Eliminating 3 chronic performance mistakes
- Adapt proven marketing strategies to your
  personal style, creating highly visible and
  compelling local prospect attraction
- Design and execute a six-month performance
  plan.

This six-month coaching program includes:

- Two one-day, face to face, personalized coaching
  sessions for top producers.
- Monthly telephone coaching sessions (group of 7)
- On-call personal one-on-one telephone coaching
- Accountability and ideas when you need them
- A step-by-step work-manual with proven tools
  that you can customize and implement
  immediately
- 4 CDs filled with top producer marketing
  highlights and tips that you can adapt to your
  own style - proven to boost sales (maybe double!)

Proven Benefits:

- You will make more money in less time
- You will open new and bigger cases consistently
- You will access affluent clients in a welcomed way
- You will maximize your revenue producing
  activities and time to sell
- You will maximize your local reputation
- You will increase your own personal satisfaction